THE ART OF THE PLAN

THE ART OF THE PLAN

A Guide to Financial Success . . . So You Can Play More!

NANCY L. BECK

Niche Pressworks

Indianapolis

THE ART OF THE PLAN

ISBN:
eBook 978-1-952654-33-6
Paperback 978-1-952654-34-3
Hardback 978-1-952654-35-0

Nancy Beck is registered with J.W. Cole Financial and J.W. Cole Advisors. Securities offered through J.W. Cole Financial, Inc. (JWC) Member FINRA/SIPC. Advisory services offered through J.W. Cole Advisors, Inc. Opinions expressed in this publication are those of the author. They do not purport to reflect the opinions or views of J.W. Cole Financial or J.W. Cole Advisors (JWCA). Beck Financial Strategies, Niche Pressworks, and JWC/JWCA are unaffiliated entities.

For permission to reprint portions of this content or for bulk purchases, contact Nancy Beck at nancy.beck@beckfs.com.

Artwork and illustrations by Nancy L. Beck

Published by Niche Pressworks; http://NichePressworks.com

"Life is a great big canvas, and you should throw all the paint on it you can."
—Danny Kaye

DEDICATION

I'D LIKE TO first dedicate this book to my mother and father, who will never see my dream realized, but whose unconditional love and support are still ever-present.

Mom, for your eternal optimism in teaching me that you "can do anything you set your mind to," and for being a steadfast listener. You have always been my #1 supporter, and every day, I can still hear your encouraging words. You truly were a Renaissance woman yourself, and your humble inspiration continues to support my voracious appetite for learning more, always.

Dad, for your dedication to our family and for introducing us to the love of good food. Some of our best times together were when sharing marvelous meals with friends and family around our dinner table. You understood the craft of making people feel at home at any meal served around the ever-welcoming Beck family dinner table. My hope is to honor you by continuing this tradition.

And last but certainly not least, I dedicate this book to my husband, John White. Your unwavering support and commitment have provided me with the courage to believe in myself and take the risks necessary to grow. You took this journey with me every step of the way, even creating the title, *The Art of the Plan*. Without your wisdom, encouragement, and our long evening discussions over a glass of wine, this book might never have been written.

CONTENTS

Part 2: THE EASY BFS WAY

Part 3: NOW FOR THE "GO-GO YEARS"

"Live as if you were to die tomorrow. Learn as if you were to live forever."
—Gandhi

ART AND FINANCE – NOT MAGIC

SOME YEARS AGO, I read the book *Start with Why* by Simon Sinek. He dedicates his writings to inspiring people to do things that inspire themselves, an idea that changed the way I look at everything I do in my own life. While *Start with Why* was written mainly for company leaders who wanted to find purpose for their businesses, it resonated with me as a message that I 1) needed to live by and 2) wanted to inspire others to live by.

The question of "why" is BIG. To many, it is abstract, overwhelming, and sometimes difficult to uncover. It had been missing in my life, and I realized I had also missed it all together when exploring my clients' lives. After my own purpose became clearer, I became more confident in sharing who I really was and what I was really about.

This helped me immensely when assisting my clients in finding their own "why," which needed to be the nucleus to building any financial plan. It also brought the enjoyment that I had been missing, the intimacy I had wished for, and the lasting friendships I now have with my clients. And maybe most life changing, it gave me the courage to share my *other side*, something I never did before.

For many years I kept my "art life" separate from my "financial planning life." I didn't think they belonged together. People would say to me how rare it was to be a financial advisor and an artist. We were supposed to be either left-brained or right-brained, but not both. When I mentioned this to my aunt, Rosemary Browne Beck, a very accomplished oil painter, she disagreed. "I don't think it is odd at all," she asserted. "Portrait painting is merely getting to know your subject; then it's all detailed problem-solving. Isn't that what you do for your clients?"

I came to understand that she was exactly right. I also began to see a theme between the two "mediums." At my studio shows, people would often say to me, "I couldn't possibly do that; you just have such talent. I can't even draw a straight line." At which I would always reply, "I can't draw a straight line either; that is what a ruler is for. Straight lines aren't that interesting, anyway."

I would hear similar sentiments in my office. "You have talents that I'll never possess. You must be gifted in calculating facts and figures. I am intimidated by it all and couldn't possibly figure this out on my own." At which I would respond, "I am good at math because I use a calculator. Financial planning is merely about listening, using common sense principles, and then finding the right tools to realize *your* unique vision."

I used to watch my mother as she taught art to her young teenage students. She would encourage them by announcing, "Anyone can be good at art. It's not a talent you're born with; it's a craft you develop over time." I have come to realize she was also right. Anyone can do anything they put their minds to if they are interested and willing to commit to learn and practice.

When I decided to write this book, I discovered the similarities between painting portraits and designing "Why-focused" financial plans. I thought it might be helpful to share, step by step, the process I use to paint a portrait. Art is not magic; it is merely a process broken down into small, easy steps that eventually come together to unveil the desired image. The financial planning process is remarkably similar, taking one step at a time, letting the information come together to eventually uncover the new way of life you are seeking to find.

The other strikingly similar aspect of the two is that of getting to know my subjects. There is an intimacy that begins to build over time. Whether it is the eyes suddenly evolving from mere brushstrokes of paint on canvas or the face looking back at me as if to say, "This is who I am," the discovery is always heart-stopping.

This emotion strikes me every single time I develop a plan and present the solutions that support my clients' own personal "Why." When I see the light begin to shine in their faces, I know I've nailed it. Their passion is truly my purpose.

INTRODUCTION

When I first begin a portrait, I research in detail the subject I am about to paint. I look at photos, read social media posts, and interview family members and friends, particularly if I have never met the person I am about to paint. I want to know more than what this person looks like. I want to know who they are (or were) and what their true passions are. What gives them joy? How do they see the world, and how would they like to be seen if portrayed in a portrait?

The same holds true when I meet a potential client for the first time. I first must uncover the vision of their ideal life and find the roadblocks that may be holding them back from their dreams. Before I can begin the process of planning, I must listen, explore, and learn who they are.

INTRODUCTION

You're Invited

"It was an insanely wonderful day!"

NONE OF US could even stop to take a sip of our wine or a bite of our food as we sat under the stars, around a table lit only by candlelight. We were mesmerized by the story of Sam's day. He was telling us about how he had awoken at 5:30 a.m. only to decide to walk to the White Street Pier to view the new year's first sunrise. Something had seemed different today for Sam. He felt invigorated, like today was going to be special.

Sam is a successful attorney, published author, and political speechwriter. He is very modest and soft-spoken about this side of himself, a side most of us had little knowledge of when we first started to get together for our monthly dinner parties.

We mainly knew he had worked hard for many years and had just recently decided to retire.

"When I got to the pier," he went on, *"I discovered a woman playing a soft classical piece on her violin, totally in sync with the upcoming sunrise. To my left, I saw a man with his dog, taking photos of the sky and the brilliant clouds that were beginning to change colors. Up ahead, I found a group of bicyclists just starting off for their daily morning ride. As I looked around, I realized I am one of them! I can be anyone I want to be today!"*

We knew Sam had been extraordinarily successful in his career but did not know the level of passion he had for music. We actually had never seen this animated side of Sam. He is—or was—a rather reserved man. He invited us into his small Key West bungalow, where we gathered around his rare upright antique Steinway piano in his modest living room. And then, he began to play.

Envision your own dinner table with the people and experiences you'd like to have around it.

The sound that his fingers made as they danced on the piano keys filled our hearts and souls with a sense of awe. It wasn't the first classical piece he had written, but it was his most ebullient. He played it with a focus that had not been there in his previous debuts. We all understood. It was *his* day. The day he finally gave himself permission to go where he had not gone before, to do things he had not done in the same way before. He had finally given himself permission to start his new way of life, doing the things he loved.

For many at our dinner party, this evolution had already taken place. We understood Sam's enlightenment and the joy that comes with it. I felt very honored to be at this gathering, as I had not yet retired. But my husband, who is eighteen years older than I, had.

In fact, we are living and planning for two retirements. Mine will not come for some time; however, I have been fortunate enough to learn how to see life differently much earlier than most my age. It has given me a greater appreciation for the real meaning of what life should be and what role money should play in it.

My hope is that this book will awaken you to a new way of thinking about the role your money can play in your life. I hope this will inspire you to consider new opportunities, instilling a new "Play More" attitude.

Financial security is paramount to giving yourself permission to start enjoying the fruits of your labor. So, this book will begin to introduce you to an easy, three-step process that will give you peace of mind that you have the solutions in place that will provide financial security, while freeing up your time for what is really important to you and your family. In other words, *Plan More to Play More.*

So, come on in! Join us! Become a guest at our table. Or better yet, set your own dinner table and surround yourself with friends and family who support your sentiments. Tell us: What would you want to be known for? How would you like to be remembered? What life experiences do you still want to share with your family and friends? And if you're not there yet, what is holding you back from living the life that you deserve?

If We Can Do It, So Can You
So, how did *we* get invited to that dinner table, and more importantly, how can you?

My husband John's and my transition started due to what we thought at the time was a crisis. We now know *that* event, the event that we "weren't ready for," was really our lifesaving event. As the saying goes, we made lemonade out of lemons. But it took some conscious effort and a real change in our mindsets. I now often say, "That was the best thing that ever happened to us. We now don't waste a good crisis; we strive to learn from it."

When John was still working, our lives were ... well, planned. He would get up every Monday morning and fly out to some city where he met with his distributors and helped them plan their next sales campaign. I was working sixty hours per week, seeing clients in my office. When I wasn't at the office, I was educating employee groups about the benefits of wise investing and planning for retirement. My day started at 7:00 a.m. and ended at 7:00 p.m.

John would fly home on Friday afternoons, tired and road weary. We'd spend the weekend catching up on home chores, sneaking in a few more hours of work. If we had the energy, we would sometimes manage to have dinner with friends.

One such Friday, John returned home from a long week in Canada and announced that his company was being sold and that all the employees would be losing their jobs. John was sixty-six, and I was forty-eight. Ironically, we hadn't talked about what we'd do in retirement. In our current life, we knew what was expected; it was on autopilot with each day already planned. While we knew that someday we'd face some challenges due to our age difference, we hadn't thought it would happen this fast.

John was tired of getting on airplanes. While he loved the business relationships he had built and the companies he helped succeed, he was ready to consider retirement. I, on the other hand, was at the height of my career and had much more I wanted to achieve in my business. I had built lasting relationships with people who depended on me, and I was not ready to stop working.

We first realized that we needed to look at things differently and really assess what we'd like to do in this next phase of our life together. I knew that if I were honest, I was beginning to burn out working such long hours and that if I were going to continue with my career, I would need to make it more flexible so that we could enjoy some of the things we wanted to.

We knew we needed to *Play More* and come up with a "Play List" of things we wanted to do. That wasn't so easy at first. **Mentally shifting gears from working to playing was foreign to us. It was overwhelming.** After working as long and hard as we had, getting to know who we were as people who could start having fun was going to take some time and planning.

In the end, we decided that some of our Play List would evolve as we started adapting to our new lives. It was OK that we didn't have everything mapped out as specifically as our work life had been. But we did know that carving out precious time was the first thing we needed to focus on.

We also started to look at our finances in a different way. We were fortunate in that we had enough money for John to retire. We had worked hard, saving our money and investing wisely. We had prepared for the "what if" scenarios of premature death and possible future long-term care expenses. But what we hadn't done was look at the spending phase of our plan. **It was not that easy to give ourselves permission to start spending some of our hard-earned savings. Even though the projections said we could, our mindset took a little more convincing.**

We told our families about our plans and committed ourselves to having a "State-of-Affairs" meeting at the end of each year. We would not only look at whether our finances and projections remained on track, but also, we'd consider our play time for the year. Where we needed help and expertise, we hired our own advisors.

In the years that followed, our lives have become more balanced and fulfilling. John is now a Master Gardener, an avid cycler, and a HAM radio operator. I began to pursue a hidden interest in art. We took time to travel and found a charming town on an island in southern Florida named Key West. We took to the energizing lifestyle where your bicycle was your main source of transportation and where arts and music were ever-present.

But maybe more importantly, we are now integral members of our community. We get to attend dinner parties with people like us, who yearn for something more. The relationships we've built are based on sharing meaningful and inspiring learning experiences that we all can celebrate together. I've come to understand that these types of attitudes and situations are rare.

The real epiphany for me was realizing that whether you're retired or not, it is important to think about money as a mechanism to be used to provide not only financial security but meaningful life experiences. The sooner a person becomes aware of what brings them pleasure and personal happiness, the more successful their retirement years will be.

Today I encourage clients to find both the time and the money to start enjoying their lives now, while they are working. Then when they retire, they will be not only financially ready but also (possibly more importantly) *emotionally* ready to live the lives they want to live.

There Is Always a Way

Often when I meet with clients, they at first seem distraught, overwhelmed, and concerned that they will not be able to do what they want in retirement. Without a plan, that may be true. But taking a few minutes to consider your wish list and then finding an expert to handle the details gives you the confidence that you can live the life you want. **During my many years working in this field, we have always found a way.** If John and I can do it with our unique circumstances, you can, too. It just takes a vision and a little planning.

My hope is that this book will be the crossroads to your realization that you deserve to live the life you choose and that you don't have to have all the answers. In fact, unless you are an expert in all of the elements of financial planning, it's best to delegate the discovery of solutions to your team of advisors. They will give you the answers you need to make informed decisions that will make sense for you and your family. **Whether you're a beginner or more of a savvy expert, the real challenge is to become an expert at knowing what you want in life, not on how you're going to get there.**

Frequently, anxiety comes when you are not sure what you've missed or even what questions to ask. And with worry comes lost days and numerous distractions that eventually consume you and cause you to think you don't even have time to consider your ideal life. It's like starting a portrait before you have a subject or building a house without first knowing what activities it needs to center around for its inhabitants.

I understand clearly that no one person can be an expert in all of the complexities of financial planning. Our process relies upon the skills of many vetted experts we bring to the table. We have what I like to call the "Under-One-Roof Planning Team." Speaking as your team ambassador, I can assure you that having access to qualified experts in each field brings confidence and stability to the plan.

With almost forty years of experience as a financial advisor and educator for numerous employer groups, charitable organizations, and associations on financial planning, I find that the process needs to be simplified to provide real value. It is not enough just to educate and motivate the people I serve; it needs to be life changing.

The BFS Way

We can move forward in achieving your dreams by taking three easy actions. We call these steps the BFS Way.

- We first **Begin with You**, finding your vision for the future while gathering information on your present financial position. This step is where you will participate the most in getting clarity about what you want and why you want it. We then need to establish your starting point in getting you there.

- Next, we **Find and Implement Solutions.** That is where you sit back and

let us find the best ways to help you create a plan customized for and in tune with your beliefs, values, and life vision. There may be several potential actions, and it is our job to clarify all of the solutions available. Then, empowered with knowledge and confidence, you make your own decisions.

- And finally, we **Stay Connected**. It is imperative that we continue communicating with you so that your plan is always in line with your life's needs. Life is fluid and unpredictable, and unless your plan stays coordinated with those changes, it could become ineffective or unsustainable.

- Staying connected also pertains to your connection with your loved ones, the people who will be directly impacted by your financial planning decisions. You'll need to provide them with information such as lists of passwords, advisors to contact, and an important document-locator list when you are not able to give them this information in person.

PART 1

YOU CAN HAVE THE LIFE YOU WANT

"If the times don't demand the best from you, invent other times".
—Unknown

CHAPTER 1

*When beginning a portrait, I typically start with the left eye. I do not merely
paint a semicircle, but rather, I begin with painting shapes exactly as they appear.
I focus on one shape at a time, connecting each with the next until together, they
begin to resemble an eye. I then move to the right eye and do the same until I
instinctively stop and step away from the canvas. In front of me unfolds the birth,
the first introduction between myself, the interpreter, and the person
coming into focus on the canvas.*

*As with painting, when beginning in a relationship with a new client,
I want to start getting more deeply into the details. Many of the questions I ask
are meant to uncover the true desires, beliefs, and worries that they possibly
have never expressed to anyone before. I like to take time to step back and look
carefully for clues that will enable me to build a plan
that will uniquely fit their vision.*

CHAPTER 1

It's OK to Want More

Take a New Perspective

I COULDN'T BELIEVE my eyes! I had done it! The image in front of me—the image I  had drawn—looked like an old man, and a rather interesting old man at that! The amazing thing was, I did not know that I was drawing an old man at all. I had merely drawn what I saw in a photograph of something unrecognizable that my instructor had taped to the corner of my easel.

What I didn't realize was that my teacher had taped the image there *upside down*. When she asked me to turn my drawing and the taped image right-side-up, I was dumbfounded as both the photo and drawing in front of me came to life. What I had copied as merely a combination of darks and lights and shapes had become a man with his chin resting in his hands, looking back at me as if to say, "You found me!"

That was the moment I realized I could be a financial advisor *and* an artist. I had never been so excited, renewed, and just downright euphoric about my next possibilities. I also realized that this energy and depth could help others find the same realization, and from that point on, I expanded my life to include art.

There is Renaissance in all of us.

That epiphany happened for me in 2003 when I was in my early forties. I often liken my experience to that of someone walking around in the attic of a house they had lived in for over forty years. In my mental "attic," in a corner amid the boxes and memorabilia stacked neatly away, lay a loose floorboard that squeaked when stepped on. One day, the board popped out slightly as if to say, "Pull me up and see what's inside." I couldn't ignore it any longer. Under the board, shimmering in plain sight, was a diamond—*my* "Hope Diamond," *my* new inspiration, *my* Art.

We all have Hope Diamonds—talents and experiences yet to be uncovered—in our mental/spiritual attics. I was not the most talented student in that art class. But I was highly likely the most inspired, and at that moment, it was life changing. I also had a perceptive teacher who saw my eyes wide open with wonder and stepped in at just the right moment to encourage and give me the permission I needed to pursue something more in my life. Had I first seen what the outcome was supposed to be— that I was assigned the daunting task of drawing a person—I am sure I would have been much more intimidated, and the outcome may have been very different.

This is what I want for you. I want to help you get to your dream. I want to believe in your vision and help you write *your* story. And most importantly, I want the BFS Way to help eliminate your fears and distractions. Together, we will produce a financial roadmap that will eventually lead you to find your own Hope Diamond.

Why Wait to Start Planning for Your Ideal Life?

Wouldn't it be much clearer if we could see into our futures? Then we'd know just how long we'd have to do the things we always wanted to do and just how long we'd need to plan for our money to last. But there is no crystal ball because life doesn't work that way. And would we really want to know exactly when we were going to die, or how our futures would turn out? Especially if we couldn't change the outcome? Probably not.

If you're intimidated by the thought of allowing yourself to do something new, maybe it's time to look at your situation differently, possibly *upside down*, first.

- This will help you begin to see your future in a different light, a future you can gain inspiration from and resolve to methodically plan for.

- When the time is right, the ideal image will appear accurate, exciting, and likely surprising in some unexpected ways.

- When you're finished, you may see yourself in the mirror, *right-side up*, saying, *"You found me."*

So, the opportunity is big to plan for the life you really want now. There are so many tools today that can help you plan for what makes you happy. No guilt, no worry. It's about getting the best there is to offer. Time is not infinite. **Success comes with having a financial plan that gives you the confidence and freedom to spend your time with family and friends on things you want to do.**

No one *wants* to do a financial plan, just as no one wants to go to the doctor or dentist. But we do because we know it is the healthy thing to do and that with reg-ular checkups, we can stave off problems that could arise into something more devastating.

According to the *Invest in You Savings Survey*, only 17 percent of Americans manage their money with the help of a financial advisor. 31 percent of Americans ages sixty-five and up use a financial advisor, compared to just 4 percent of Americans ages eighteen to twenty-four, and 7 percent of Americans ages twenty-five to thirty-four.[1] So, it appears that we get wiser (or maybe just less confident) as we get closer to retirement or as we see how complicated and unpredictable life can really be.

Having no financial advisor can prove to be expensive. Based on a study done by DALBAR from 1990 to 2010, the unmanaged S&P 500 Index earned an average of 7.81 percent annually. Over that same period, the average "do-it-yourself-er" equity investor earned only 3.49 percent annually![2]

Over twenty years, that would have meant an investment starting at $100K would have grown to nearly $450K if compounded at 7.81 percent, while at 3.49 percent, it only grew to $198.6K. The difference in performance had more to do with the inability to manage emotions, often causing investors to buy when the market was high and sell when the market was low, than with the mild differences in a mutual fund's performance.

We now have unprecedented access to investment information with detailed security statistics and real-time news information online. While this has leveled the playing field between Wall Street and Main Street, this information does not provide enlightenment on how this applies to your own unique situation. And although you are constantly encouraged to "do it yourself," can you really manage your own investments as well as a professional, and without the assistance of a paid advisor? And more importantly, do you want to?

If you're constantly anxious about money, do you truly feel you are objective enough to create a financial plan that allows you to find the time to start "playing more"? Are you completely assured that in "going it alone" you are definitely not missing anything important that a professional financial advisor would catch? As with anything, if we are too close to the situation, we most likely do not have the unbiased, clear perspective that we should.

Investment choices are so much more complicated today. Asset allocation is just one component of sound money management. Maybe it's time to delegate the research and details to a professional who can fill you in on the facts that pertain to your personal situation. You then can be confident that the decisions you make are sound and that you are not missing a key component that could throw all your plans off track.

Take This Opportunity to Do It Right

Build In Your Security

Life involves many things you need to worry about. When you know that you and your advisor have covered all the right bases, you will then have the confidence to spend some of your hard-earned nest egg. Everyone seems to have a different number/dollar amount in mind that would make them feel financially secure. So, what is your number, and why?

To be financially independent really means not having to work for a living unless, of course, you want to. It would mean that you have enough investment income to cover all your living expenses into perpetuity.

One popular online formula to finding your financial independence target is to take the number of years left in your life, multiplied by your current living expenses. The sum would be the amount you would need to be financially independent. For example, if you have a nest egg of $3M and thirty years left to live, you could be financially independent if your living expenses are no more than $100K a year.

But there is more to this than meets the eye.

First, you may want to start doing some of your Play More items before you retire, weaving these experiences into your life while also saving for retirement. In the early 1900s it was rare for people to live much past the age of sixty-five. Today we are living much longer, and our aspirations have changed. We want to enjoy some life now, finding interests and meaning before retirement, while still feeling secure that we are on track to have a successful retirement.

Second, there are big flaws with the $3M/$100K formula. Where is inflation in this calculation? What about earnings? How would these two variables change your outlook? And what about other income sources you would be receiving, such as a pension or social security, that would reduce the amount you would need in your nest egg?

And most importantly, how do you know something won't go wrong? **It is not easy to overcome the fear of not working.** We need to be able to believe in the data and stay in tune to alter the plan accordingly year after year, as curveballs come our way. And they will.

The answers to these questions are not in a one-size-fits-all formula. It is as individualized as painting a portrait reflecting all your unique features and characteristics. Confidence that your plan fits the unique needs of you and your family is paramount to your sense of security.

Avoid Unnecessary Losses

Avoiding losses can be more important than making gains. An understanding financial advisor—who stays in touch and is accessible when you need to just talk things out or vet your fears—is priceless. The cost of a wrong move can be more devastating than the cost of your advisor's advice, especially if that advice focuses on

keeping you on track and unemotional. **At times, a financial advisor's role is to walk you back from the proverbial cliff.**

When Sarah and Judy first came into our office, they were newly retired and feeling very anxious about managing their own money. They had a broker with whom they'd spoken only a few times over the last five years. The last time they had all discussed their situation in detail, Judy and Sarah were still working, had good incomes, and felt confident about their 50 percent equity/50 percent bond allocation.

But things had changed. They hadn't informed their broker about their early retirement plans or their newfound concern around the recent political news and market conditions. In the spring of 2020, they decided to move all their holdings into cash even though their portfolio was down over 15 percent. They wanted their fear to stop.

Today, we are working to bring this portfolio back. That year, they had a substantial 13 percent loss, which they could have avoided if they had had someone to lean on—someone to discuss their fears and the pros and cons of the action they were considering. While they may have made the same decision, they would not have felt so "lost and alone," as they put it.

If they had stayed faithful to their customized, long-term plan, their portfolio could have been up as much as 11 percent that year.[3] While the results don't always work out that way, **when emotions drive actions related to money, the outcome is often disheartening and expensive.**

Have Peace of Mind

Peace of mind can exist on many levels. On one hand, it is a sense that you are making the right choices for yourself and your family. On another, it comes from knowing you haven't missed an imperative component to your financial well-being.

And what about peace of mind for your loved ones? If you are the one reading this book, logic has it that you are likely the one who does the planning. It is on your shoulders; the final responsibility is yours. Or at least that is what you might tell yourself.

But what if your spouse or significant other wants to be involved but doesn't know how to ask? Maybe they are intimidated by the money or by you. They may believe that if they ask, you might feel they are infringing on your territory.

One of my clients, Chris, felt that way. He never showed his checkbook to his wife or children. He always paid the bills and divvied out money, when asked, for family expenses. His wife Maggie never complained to him but quietly started her own financial plan. It wasn't that she didn't trust her husband or that he didn't provide enough; she just felt very vulnerable. She didn't know how to talk with him about their money, and she wanted to be educated and have a plan if something ever happened to him.

As we worked with her over the years, she built up a nice portfolio of her own. She owned her own art supply business and understood profit and loss statements and even started a retirement plan for her employees.

Eventually, she encouraged Chris to join us in our financial planning sessions, and he grew to enjoy the experience. He told me often that he didn't know how to talk about money with Maggie, and they both began to make good financial decisions together. When Chris retired, *they* decided on which pension benefit to take. *They* planned for long-term care expenses, updated their wills, and pre-planned their funeral services.

Some years later when Chris passed, Maggie had a plan, one that they both had shared with their three children. Chris's death brought great sadness and grief, but no fear. Chris and Maggie had shown one another and their children a great act of love. The planning of their estate, the organizing of their belongings, and the recording of their wishes made the process of executing their estate seamless and worry-free.

Play More and Worry Less
So, what about you? Isn't it time to start thinking about your Play List? If not now, when? When would there be a better time to start delegating the tasks that you aren't trained to do and really, if honest, don't want to do?

What really makes you happy? What are the top five things on your Play List? What is keeping you from starting to do the things you want to do? Do you not deserve them? Do you need permission—from yourself, others, your advisor?

The Myth about Worry
Worry can be an addiction founded on a false perception. "If I'm worried, then I am thinking about my money," you may believe. "If I am thinking about my money, then I am working on my money. If I am working on my money, then I am making it grow."

Not so; you are just worrying and stuck in a cycle of analysis-paralysis. Not knowing which way to go is maddening. It is safer to do nothing. It feels better to just keep doing what you've been doing, even though it is not clear what you are accomplishing.

Doing it alone has its advantages. You don't have to figure out what makes you happy. You have a built-in reason to live. You have a full-time job, along with your other full-time job. You are being a good provider for your family, or so you tell yourself. But what if there is a better way?

The BFS Way

"BFS" obviously stands for the initials of my company name, Beck Financial Strategies, but I also like to *coin* our process the "Built for Success" Way. **The BFS Way gives you peace of mind and ease of management.** But first, you must believe that you deserve to start spending your money on the life you want to live. The BFS Way starts with three easy steps.

1. Begin with You

We first want to help you find your own "Why," your Play List of experiences yet to be discovered. What are these things? When do you want to do them? How will the people that are important to you benefit from your wishes? I would encourage you to stop here and consider these questions. You will find all of the resources referenced in this book on the Bonus page of

our website at **BeckFS.com/Bonus.8.htm.** It might be fun to start dreaming a little about what your new life could be.

2. Find and Implement Solutions

Then we build a money strategy that will take into account the six components of a complete financial plan to mold around the life you want to live. These components include Cash Management, Insurance, Tax, Investment, Retirement, and Estate Planning.

3. Stay Connected

You will continue to stay connected to your dreams and your plan. One process brings in both the aspects of your Financial Plan and your Play List.

You Deserve to Delegate the Hard Stuff

It is time to take a fresh look at how you would like to spend the rest of your days. You deserve to have access to an easy-to-use financial planning platform for gathering and maintaining up-to-date data. You deserve to have an expert who will oversee your investments and total financial picture and be informed when changes need to be made. You deserve to delegate the tasks of keeping up with all of the changes in new tax laws, economic and market conditions, and estate-planning regulations that could impact your financial plan. And last, you deserve to turn your nest egg into a time-segmented, income-producing vehicle that is finally working for you.

CHAPTER 2

When getting to know the subject I am painting, I want to be sure I portray them doing something they love. It is often hard for the viewer to get to know the person in the painting just by looking at a face staring back at them. But if the subject is focused on something or someone they love, and that interaction can be realistically portrayed, well then, we are now introduced to a more meaningful character on the canvas.

It is not money that makes a person interesting or even successful.
It is what they do with their time that really brings depth to their character.
In painting a portrait, it is my job to portray this as accurately as possible.
As a financial advisor, it is my job to uncover what really matters to my client,
then remove as many distractions as possible so they can spend
their valuable time doing those things.

CHAPTER 2

The Real Value Is Time

It's about *Your* Time

WAYNE HAD A GOOD LIFE. He was healthy, had two grown children, and had a wife who had been with him over forty-five years and whom he loved dearly. They lived in an upscale neighborhood, and both had monthly pensions, Social Security, and more than enough money saved for their retirement years.

But Wayne was constantly at his computer all hours of the day and night, logging in to check on his money. He was never happy with the returns his portfolio made, even in excellent years. He was always comparing his results to indexes that had nothing to do with the needs and objectives of his own portfolio. He was searching for unattainable returns. After two short years, he instructed me to change money managers because he

thought the *grass looked greener on the other side*. Had he stayed where he originally was, he would have had better performance over the long run.

He had talked with me about his buddies that he met for breakfast every morning, earning "double-digit returns year after year," and wondered why he was not. He and his wife have always been somewhat risk-averse, so while his portfolio was designed for lower volatility and income, his mindset was still that he should be earning "to the moon" returns. And for what? So that he could log in and see he made a good return the day before? How was that improving his life?

I had come to an impasse with Wayne and suggested that maybe I was not helping him at all. He was rather surprised and said he didn't know what I meant and that he was quite happy with our relationship. I suggested that he was losing precious time looking over his money and that at age seventy-nine, he might have many unrealized Play List items that he and his family have not yet experienced. I suggested to him that they would likely never spend all their money, and instead of enjoying the fruits of their labors, he was wasting away at his computer desk frustrated and alone much of the time.

A few weeks later, Wayne called and told me he had started spending more time at his church volunteering (something he had not done before), and he and his wife had planned a trip to Europe. He said that for the first time, he was enjoying his life so much more and even began riding his bike again. He also told me that he limited his "account login time" to once per week. At the end of our conversation, with his voice wavering a bit, he thanked me and said, "Nancy, I now see that the real value of having *you* is the time I now have for *my family and me.*"

Be an expert on your ideal life; hire an expert to help you realize it.

Sometime later, Wayne's wife sent me a note to thank me. She did not know what had transpired or what I had said to her husband, but she felt that his transformation had resulted from our last meeting. I would suggest that his new way of thinking came when he realized his previous focus had not filled his soul and that now, while he was still taking care of his family, he was doing so in a way that he did not have to micromanage.

THE VALUE IS TIME
*The value of having you is the
time I now have for me.*

What Exactly Is Financial Planning?

Let's take a few minutes to talk about the terms "Financial Planning" or "Wealth Management" because there are a lot of misconceptions around what they really mean. To many, it is investment management. To some, it means you must have a lot of money to partake in the benefits. For others, it just sounds like a lot of work, and the information that you receive is not helpful or meaningful to you. You may just be stuck because you have some of these preconceived notions in your head ... or maybe it's a totally new concept.

Most advisors use financial planning as a tool to merely draw you in to manage your money. Advisors often require an investment minimum that you must meet in order for them to talk with you. That right there should tell you that it is not about you, but rather it's about how much money you are able to invest. With this approach, the plan they offer is most often a one-size-fits-all approach to your financial situation.

BFS LIFE Plan

The terms most used to describe this process are either Financial Planning or Wealth Management. I use a more encompassing description. **Built for Success: Lasting Interactive Financial Enrichment Planning,** or the **BFS LIFE Plan.**

What the **BFS LIFE Plan** does is first explore in detail the "Why" in your life planning. What are *your* aspirations, *your* fears, and your yet-to-be-lived Play List? Why have you made past decisions, and what were your perceived "wins and losses"? What makes you worry and feel insecure? What builds your confidence and brings you peace? And what do you want to achieve by partaking in the BFS LIFE Planning Process?

Many who have tried working with other financial planners have noted the process lacked much of the BFS first step.

BFS LIFE Plan—Built for Success

- **L**asting

- **I**nteractive

- **F**inancial

- **E**nrichment

The data gathering almost immediately focused solely on the financials. How much do you have in investable assets? When do you want to retire? Do you have life insurance? Tell us about your income (not so much about your debt). And they never want to delve into your spending plan as that is way too much work for the reward.

The BFS Way first gathers information to have a clear picture of who you are and what you want. Then, the data gathering and foundational planning come into play. We, too, must acquire the facts and figures and begin to assess and then inform you about your present position. We always prepare a spending plan, as that is the bedrock to knowing the income that you will need for the life you want to live. We must build the foundation from an accurate beginning to attain the objectives over the long term.

You may have tried financial planning and failed to see the value. You may have received recommendations without your advisor even diving into what you really want your money to do for you. In fact, your advisor may not have known you at all. The recommendations seemed to come out of a cookie-cutter list where they mentioned something like, "Save more for retirement." "Have three to six months of expenses put away for emergencies." Or "Buy more life insurance." In fact, the plan may have been more in line with your planner's best interest than that of your own.

Why DIY-ers Don't Have Fun

So, like Wayne, many try the do-it-your-self (DIY) approach. The problem with this approach is that, as I mentioned before, it can have a lot of costly and emotionally damaging pitfalls. If you are not an expert at all the key components such as tax, risk, retirement, investment, and estate planning, you are bound to miss something. For DIY-ers, the job becomes full-time, whether they want it to be or not. They must keep up with the ever-changing tax laws and economic conditions that can affect their plan. And what if something happens to you? Does your family know your system? Do they have the skills necessary to carry on what you started?

Another pitfall is acquiring advice from friends, family, or even your retirement plan representative at work. While they mean well, they have no inkling about your financial situation or risk tolerance when it comes to investing. They most likely do not know your cash flow habits and income needs. And many are in denial and have made bad choices for themselves over the years. What works for them will not be the relevant and appropriate solution for you, even if they were lucky enough to have good results.

And the most important pitfall is that while you are trying to do it all yourself, alone on the computer, precious moments are passing you by. **Most DIY-ers are not as confident as they appear.** Because of this, they are always checking and rechecking their work, often spending more time looking for what they missed or for what action should be taken next. Often emotions can take the place of objective decision-making, which causes more stress and costly mistakes. And all along the way, the family and friendship time is taking a back seat.

A good plan must be designed to support your vision while at all times providing financial security and ease of management. The answers are clear. They fit exactly around what you are seeking in your life. There may be compromises—there usually are—but all are shaped with a conscious effort to provide you with the confidence and the time to enhance your and your family's life experiences.

So, is the cost of a good advisor worth it? Maybe, if your advisor has ever walked you back from a cliff when almost making a costly emotional decision. Or possibly, if you would have missed that new tax law changing how you should take funds out of an IRA to avoid penalties. And most definitely, if it allows you to spend more time with loved ones, creating memories that will last for generations to come.

CHAPTER 3

Sometimes when I paint a portrait, I want to focus on the power of the character. I want to keep away any distractions that may deter the viewer from seeing "what's inside" the person looking back at them.

Many people are embarrassed to have a portrait painted of themselves. It may seem narcissistic or too personal. It may uncover something they don't like about themselves. But for many who love that character on the canvas, they often see a much "brighter light" than the subject may see in themselves.

As with working with a client in building a plan for their ideal life, I look for their potential as well as their reality. There is always more than what meets the eye, and it is my duty to help uncover what that is.

Give Yourself Permission to Make a Change

There Is No Time Like the Present

"I JUST CAN'T BELIEVE this happened to me!" Jim said. He held his head in both hands, elbows leaning on the table as if the weight of the news was just too heavy to comprehend. He was staring at the figure on his 401(k) statement, a figure that had been 60 percent higher three months ago. "How could this have happened?"

I met Jim some years earlier while teaching a "Pathways to Retirement" workshop for a local company. I had worked one-on-one with the employees of this company for many years. I knew the company culture and their 401(k) plan. I also knew that most felt "well informed" about their own company stock and how it was performing.

They often would hold all of their 401(k) funds in the company stock, even receiving the matching contributions in the same stock. They were confident that they would be the first to know if there was *bad news in the air* because they worked there.

From time to time, rumors would surface, and they would sell their stock and transfer their funds to the fixed account also offered within the plan. This was a back-and-forth process that seemed to work for them, as most felt they were earning a decent return on their portfolios, despite their lack of investment knowledge.

During a program break, Jim came up to me with great confidence and stated, "I really loved your presentation! Once my

Waiting to make a change when you know your plan is too risky can cost you:

- Money

- Time

- An Earlier Retirement Date

- Worry and Anxiety

stock goes back up to $75 per share, I am going to come to you and diversify! I've known I needed to do it, but I am just waiting for the right moment."

I thanked him for his enthusiasm but suggested that **"Now just might be the right time. Especially if you know that what you are currently doing does not fit your risk tolerance or life plan. There is no time like the present."** A few months later, at great surprise to the employees, the company was sold. Within months of the sale, the stock plummeted to one-sixteenth of its previous value.

By the time Jim and his wife decided they needed help, the news was not good. Jim's 401(k) plan had diminished from almost $600,000 to less than $100,000, and

the new company had sent early retirement notices to many of the older employees, including him. They had fifteen days to decide whether to take the "deal" or risk being let go anyway with a reduced pension benefit and no health insurance.

I never again want to experience seeing the panic in someone's eyes when they realize they waited too long to get their financial plan in order. They did not see the clear and present danger that was about to seize upon them. Life is full of curveballs. Whether it is a pandemic or some other event out of our control, they all can cause devastating effects on a family's future financial security and life plan.

While we have been able to make a new, more modest retirement plan work, the process was not without anxiety and some considerable compromises. Today, Jim and his wife Sarah urge me to tell their story to everyone I can. "If we had just found you twenty years earlier. We just didn't know what we didn't know."

What's Holding You Back?

So many times, it really comes down to giving ourselves permission to implement a financial plan. We tell ourselves we do not need it or don't feel we are qualified to even consider a financial plan. Or maybe we just don't see the value of paying for a plan and think we can save money by doing it ourselves. But most often, we just procrastinate until something *makes us do it.*

Unfortunately, inaction brings a pattern of not getting the results we want. Feeling unqualified leaves us stuck, even paralyzed to act. Many have told me that secretly, they were actually craving for someone to take control of their situation and tell them what to do.

Maybe you have felt embarrassed that you don't feel you know enough to even partake in a financial plan, don't feel organized enough, or feel intimidated by what you might find if you take a hard look at your current situation. My client Ellen felt that way.

Give Yourself Permission to Live a Big Life

A few years ago, Ellen came into my office with two grocery bags of statements. She sat down at the table, looking defeated, and said, "Nancy, I don't even know where to begin!" Looking through eyes full of tears, she added, "It all just seems too overwhelming."

Ellen had been the primary caretaker for her husband Jeff for many years. He had a rare disease that caused him to have strokes which left him totally dependent on Ellen. In the early years, he had handled all of the money decisions, paid the bills, and was one of those people that could walk into a room and immediately become the center of attention. He had a big personality, but Ellen was truly the *wind beneath his wings*.

When Jeff became unable to speak or walk, Ellen needed to take over the finances, which at this point were very disorganized and at risk from all of the medical bills that were adding up. Jeff had never consulted with a financial advisor, and Ellen just didn't have any idea what the plan was, or even if there was one.

When Ellen came in for help, I knew we needed to overcome one real obstacle. Ellen had no confidence when it came to making decisions about money. She would worry, obsess, and often go to her brother-in-law for additional advice and approval.

When Ellen and I started working together, I urged her to start thinking about money as a tool to give her what she needs and financial planning as a process to target those needs. I asked her just two questions. **What are the things that matter to you most, and what are the things that you can control?** By making this process relatable and relevant, I was able to help Ellen better uncover what she wanted and needed their money to do for them. She also started to worry less as we prepared for the things she could not control and enhanced the benefits on the things she could.

My job was to educate her on available solutions and enlighten her on how they coordinated with her wishes, allowing her to feel empowered to make her own decisions. Ellen was more than qualified to make sound decisions about her money. She had a great deal of common sense, and she was clear on what she wanted and needed from her money. That is really all she needed to focus on; she could delegate the rest.

Today, Ellen is a confident woman who has found a seat at our dinner table. Since Jeff passed away three years ago,

Ellen has taken on her new way of life. She was absolutely devoted to Jeff and has no regrets. But as life would have it, she now has grown into her new identity—that of a confident, self-sufficient, world-traveling woman who teaches English to immigrants wanting to become US citizens. Even though she doesn't need to, Ellen wanted to start working again. For her, that is what felt right.

What about That Monster in the Closet?

For many of us, the "monster" gets bigger the longer we try to stave it off. What is the monster in your closet? Is it those debts you haven't looked at for a while? What about that investment that you know you need to diversify but aren't sure how? And what about the long list of accounts you have spread over two states in five previous employers' plans? What are the answers you don't want to hear? That you can't do what you want? That you will have to work longer?

Wouldn't it be better to know sooner rather than later if you are not on track to finding your dream-come-true life? We talked about this one evening at our monthly dinner party. Susie expressed her frustration about her father, who was avoiding going to the doctor because he had a sore foot. He was afraid the doctor would send him to the hospital after a myriad of tests, and he didn't want to go. "I'd rather die than go to the doctor!" she said in a deep voice, mimicking what her father had said to her earlier that day, "I'd just rather go peacefully in my easy chair!"

We all laughed a little, but in some way, we understood. "But really," Susie went on as if she were speaking to her father, "Dad, you don't get to go from sore foot to death; somewhere in between, there's amputation! Maybe you'd rather have a $10,000 foot bill than a $300,000 life-support bill. And maybe even better, you could nip the problem in the bud before it gets to be a monster and avoid all of that suffering!" She was right; there were ugly stages in between that very possibly could be avoided.

While some people defer action because they have a case of analysis-paralysis, others possess the opposite quality: passive resistance. While it can feel safer and much less terrifying to stay the course, to just plod along and hope for the best, inaction can have devastating effects. And more often than not, the monster eventually will come out anyway. The sooner you face it, the easier it is to make the uncertainty go away. In most cases, what originated in our minds as a fifteen-foot, unforgiving dinosaur ends up being a brown-eyed teddy bear.

You've Got This!

The really neat thing is you have the power. You maintain the control. And you are totally qualified to do this if you know the answer to one simple question. What do you want your ideal life to look like? Then your answer—your vision—will draw you forward.

You don't need to be a qualified money expert; the expertise you need is something you already have—knowledge of *yourself* and *your* most rewarding life. It really comes down to three things. If you Plan More, you can then Play More, which allows you to Be More.

PART 2
THE EASY BFS WAY

"Lost time is never found again."
—Benjamin Franklin

CHAPTER 4

I never met Wayne (the subject in this portrait), as he passed away before I had the opportunity of knowing him directly. But he left clues. I understood by the images left behind and the stories his family told, that he lived a big life full of adventure, artistic accomplishments, and deep affection for those he loved. He wasn't afraid of life; he embraced it.

Wayne was a different subject for me. The tattoos he sported reflected details about his outlook on life and his passions about what and who he loved. I needed to get the details precisely accurate, even down to the small "♥ you Dad" placed intimately on the inner side of his right elbow. Even though his life was cut short, I feel confident he would tell you that he had no regrets about how he lived his days.

Whether working on canvas or in the conference room, I try to uncover all of the details around the true passions that bring out the best in each person I work with. To understand what will make a successful plan, we must first focus on what is important to them, down to the last detail, even if they start out feeling that it might be trivial.

How to Play More and Worry Less

Start with the Simple Answers

STARTING THE PROCESS of financial planning didn't feel easy to Jesse. He had always done it himself; he had his own system. When he first came to me, he was resistant to letting go, and more importantly, to getting help.

Jesse had saved and worked his whole life, only taking one week's vacation per year—usually spending it catching up on home repairs. He never felt he had enough money. He never once asked himself "Why" he was saving all of this and what he wanted to do with it later.

He was merely doing what the financial gurus said he needed to do. *Work, provide for your family, invest wisely, but mostly save.* When he came to me, he was concerned that he hadn't done something right, and he worried that whatever it was, it would be BIG.

I knew that Jesse would feel better once he understood the three simple steps to get him to his answers, so I took him through the BFS LIFE Plan process.

Begin with You

The "Why"

In this step, we looked at the "Three Ws"– "Why," "What," and "When"–to help us both uncover a clearer picture of where he wanted to go. I explained that the "Why" is really the backbone, the purpose of his life, and the thing or things that might inspire him or make him happy. I relayed that this plan would not be as meaningful to

We must find your "Why" before we can move to your "What" and "When."

- You are entitled to be fulfilled by the life you want to live.

- You have the right to wake up feeling inspired and confident about your path forward.

- Your "Why" will feel more meaningful if it includes contributing to something larger than yourself.

him if he didn't have at least a rough sketch of how he'd like to see his life after he stopped working.

I knew that retirement was terribly uncomfortable for him, and he felt overwhelmed. But he was only focusing on the numbers—the nuts and bolts. He had not come to realize yet that his money needed to start working for him. He may have thought the "Why" was too personal and that it was really none of anyone's business, certainly not his financial advisor's. *What did this have to do with his money, anyway?*

When I asked him what he saw himself doing after he retired, he promptly replied, "I'd probably just do the same thing I have

been doing. I don't plan on spending any of my savings."

The challenge was that he now had eight to ten more free hours per day, which he didn't have before, and it was going to take some time for him to figure out what he would do to fill them. It would have been quite easy for someone like Jesse to fill those free hours obsessing over his money—researching, worrying about how it was growing, comparing it to indexes, and reading every article he could get his hands on. But he wouldn't spend a dime of it! I didn't want that for him. I didn't want him to miss his life.

Jesse had recently married after being single for many years. He had no children of his own, and even before delving into his details, I knew he would never spend all of his money or outlive his savings. What I hoped to accomplish was to open his mind to a new way of thinking, one that would encourage him to start living life on his own terms instead of those expressed by his past employers or the financial experts he was compelled to follow on TV and websites.

I did have one accomplice in uncovering this evolution of "Why"—Jesse's wife, Cheryl. Cheryl had been a single parent for many years. She saved well and had raised a son who now was on his own and doing well. She, too, had been conservative and had always looked at her life in a way that included her son. For the first time, she was able to start seeing herself doing things that she hadn't been able to do before, due to her responsibilities as a mom. She was open to finding her new identity but wasn't clear about how. And that was OK!

As with many, Jesse and Cheryl struggled with this first step, so we started small. We took this task apart and reduced it to baby steps.

We began with questions such as: Who are the family members you care about the most? Who are your friends, and why do you enjoy them? What brings you the most comfort or puts you in the best mood? Is it reading, or riding your motorcycle, or working on your house? Could it be eating a good meal or traveling? Also, we needed to uncover what made them lose sleep at night. What worried them and made them uncomfortable?

The "What"
We next delved into the "What." That is the easy part for some and a little harder for others, but our process streamlines it almost effortlessly. Jesse and Cheryl kept a listing of all their accounts and had their statements readily available. The one challenge was that they still were handling their day-to-day money matters as individuals and not as one family unit. He paid some bills; she paid others. But neither really knew exactly what they were spending together as a family.

We set them up with our easy online questionnaire that they could fill in at their leisure. We also got them set up with their own BFS Money Site subscription, which allowed the process to become much easier to monitor going forward. They could link any accounts via username and passwords, and then going forward, those values would update overnight automatically into their website. They could see their full financial picture in real time and in one place.

The other component of their "What" was knowing their exact income needs. To know this, they needed to understand what they were spending now. The BFS Money Site—linked to their checking, savings, and credit card accounts—tracked and categorized what they were spending. The only aspect that they would have to account for on their own was their cash spending.

The "When"

And last was the "When." When was life going to transition for them? When would Jesse really pull the trigger and retire? When would they need to start turning what they saved from an accumulation portfolio into an income-producing portfolio? And if they found some Play List items they'd like to partake in, such as traveling or starting a new hobby, when did they want to start?

I introduced the idea to Jesse and Cheryl that there are really three phases in our retirement years. I like to refer to them as the Go-Go Years, the Slow-Go Years, and the No-Go Years. And *they*, I hinted, were in their Go-Go Years. These were the years in which their health was good, and they were free to go out and do the things they really wanted to do. These were especially important years. In these years, they would make memories, share friendships, see faraway places, and grow exponentially as human beings! These were the years they'd get to live on their own terms.

I also suggested that they could plan to take additional income from their portfolio for these years, and they should. **We don't know how long the Go-Go Years will last, but once they're gone, they typically never return.**

We then, I explained, slip into our Slow-Go Years. During these years, we

THE ART OF THE PLAN

tend to stay closer to home and doctors, and if we have children, seek to live nearer to them. We tend to spend less money on the fun things but may have a few more medical bills.

And last, I added, we enter the No-Go Years. Most of us cannot avoid these years. These can be the most difficult and expensive years, and thus the BFS LIFE Plan must have contingencies in place to provide for the required cost of this stage of life. Sadly, many will forgo the Go-Go Years for fear they will not have enough money left to take care of them in the No-Go Years. That just doesn't need to be the case.

Find and Implement Solutions

Once we had all the pertinent information about what they wanted, their current financial position, and when they wanted to begin letting their money work for them, it was time for us to step in and find the way.

Now the "monkey" had been transferred to my team's back. I told Jesse and

Cheryl to sit back and relax but to continue envisioning details about their new life, especially now that they were seeing it as exciting and liberating, rather than worrisome and overwhelming as they had feared.

Income Needs First

My team and I dissected the data, looked at all of the figures objectively, all from the perspective of Jesse's and Cheryl's new life expectations. We assessed their cash flow needs first, as that was the guidepost, the leading indicator of what their portfolio and other income sources needed to do for them. Jesse and Cheryl's spending habits were exceptionally low. I typically break down cash flow needs into three categories; "Needs," "Wants," and "Desires."

"Needs" spending items describe things one can't live without: utilities, home maintenance, automobile expenses, medical and insurance payments, and basic food requirements. "Wants" spending items refer to things planned for in the future or general entertainment/lifestyle choices, such as dining out, going to the movies, or home upgrades. The "Desires" category differs from the "Wants" category in that it refers to personal, individual elements that enable self-expression or expansion or the exploration of one's creative side. These are highly individual and involve things such as hobbies, certain types of more personally motivated travel (such as spiritual pilgrimages or visiting family overseas to reestablish roots), or giving special gifts.

We could easily account for their "Needs" spending items and calculate the "Wants" spending items, but we found truly little "Desires" spending items. However, during our "Begin with You" discovery stage, we had learned that they had always wanted to travel the United States in an RV and that they also wanted to help Cheryl's only grandson with future college expenses. Therefore, we knew some of what they might want to do in relation to the "Desires" category.

Roadmap Uncovered
We then took a detailed look at exactly what assets they had, where they were

invested, and what they provided in terms of their new life wishes. We assessed how much risk or volatility each account was exposed to, how easily the investments were to manage, and the tax status of each account. And we took time to compile these in reports that would be easy to understand and follow when the time came for us to explain them to Jesse and Cheryl.

We ran reports showing how each investment would project out into their future, showing a retirement income need 25 percent greater than their cash flow statement had revealed. We wanted them to have their RV life and feel they could give generously to their grandson, as those were the things that would bring them joy and contentment in their lives.

We then assessed the risks. What pitfalls were present that could keep their ideal life from continuing to be on track? What if one of them got sick, had a need for long-term care, or even passed away earlier than expected? We needed to calculate what that meant for the survivor in terms of income need and financial security. We found a few gaps that we needed to address, but the plan was still very doable and could remain sound, even with the "Desires" spending allowance left in place.

Simple Explanations

Now it was time to share our discoveries and solutions with Jesse and Cheryl. We introduced them to their new spending plan, complete with RV and education funding. We showed them the complexities of their current investment holdings and how they were or were not currently suited for their life goals. We illustrated the "what ifs" of a premature death or long-term care crisis and how these might impact their life savings.

It was the first time that Jesse and Cheryl had looked at a net worth statement combining both of their assets. They were clearly surprised and somewhat delighted with what they had saved apart, but now together. It was a liberating moment for them both.

We shared aspects of their current position that would be cumbersome and inefficient, especially in supporting their new life vision. We explained detailed options for simplifying their lives through streamlined, tax-efficient money management. We showed them where the risks were and gave some options for managing them. And last, we covered the aspects that would help their heirs with the estate management requirements that would eventually come.

With all of that information, the end result/bottom line was this: **they could live the life they wanted and still have financial security.** I was excited for them, but when I looked up at Cheryl, I saw an emotion I had seen before but still never expect. She was trembling a bit, and her eyes were welling up with tears. Jesse saw it, too, and took her hand and asked, "What is wrong? Why the tears?" Taking the tissue I had given her, Cheryl replied, "These are tears of joy and relief. I can't believe this is *our* financial plan. I can't believe this can be our life! We can really afford an RV?"

We all laughed; it was time for some humor. I replied, "You bet you can, and just so you know, I came up with the expenses for your RV from my own experience. John and I, too, have an RV. We named it "ET." Eyes wide open in surprise, Jesse and Cheryl exclaimed, "You named your RV 'Extraterrestrial'?" "No," I replied. "Expensive Toilet!"

Take advantage of the Go-Go Years before it's too late.

Stay Connected

So, are you starting to get the picture of why I do what I do? It's less about the money and more about the life. And when we can assist with a life-changing mindset, we are all in!

But the plan is never really finished. It always needs to be tweaked and edited as life unfolds. That is why it is essential to the success of their plan that our clients stay connected with each other, with their advisors, and with those who will be eventually impacted by the decisions they make.

Stay Connected with One Another

Staying connected with each other may sound obvious, but ironically, people often don't realize they're not doing it. I often hear, "We see each other every day. Isn't that staying connected?"

"Not necessarily," I would reply. "Unless you have readdressed your life goals, planned for new Play List ideas, and remained conscious about family dynamics that may impact your previous decisions, there is still some communicating that needs to happen. And it starts first, privately, between the two of you."

Stay Connected with Your Advisors

We need to know what is working and what is not. We will always need to be brought into clients' private discussions when it impacts their financial planning. We want this plan to continue to evolve with them and their path forward.

We also must keep them abreast of the changes that could impact their plan. These would include the economic outlook, political environment, fiscal and tax policies, inflation, and estate law changes. We need to be able to communicate in clear terms how we might alter the strategies to keep them as efficient and financially sound as possible. The plan must remain up to date to succeed over the long term.

Stay Connected with Family

Jesse and Cheryl's son, Tim, was the one who would be most impacted by their financial plan. He was their executor and would have power of attorney, and he would be responsible for helping them through some tough choices as they aged. He would also be administering their estate once they had passed. It was important that we communicated both Jesse's and Cheryl's wishes to Tim and that we educated him on the vehicles we had in place that would make these things easier when the time came. Initially, Jesse and Cheryl wrote a letter specifying their final wishes. A few years later, they pre-planned their funeral arrangements so their passing would be as easy as possible for Tim.

I made the point to meet with him, Jesse, and Cheryl so that Tim knew who I was and would understand that I was working to find solutions in all their best interests. We have family meetings from time to time, and Tim eventually started to plan for his own financial future with his wife and son as well.

We then continued the process by providing Tim with access to the Vault located in their personal BFS Money Site. Cheryl and Jesse wanted Tim to have full access to their website in case they were ever incapacitated. The Vault provided them with a secure place to store all of their important documents electronically and also featured an up-to-date BFS Document Locator List so Tim would know where to find their originals. Tim greatly appreciated this aspect of their plan.

It's Just That Easy

The process was just that easy. It might have taken Jesse and Cheryl a couple of hours to compile the information we requested to build their plan. They weren't required to start writing a journal, or to learn how to paint a portrait, or to change their entire lifestyle right off the bat. In the beginning, all we needed was a brief sketch of what they might want. The rest would evolve over time.

Sadly, most professionals in our industry don't want to explore the "Why" with their clients. Maybe they themselves are not in tune with their own "Why" or purpose and just want to focus on the money, impressing you with performance measurement terms such as "Alphas" and "Betas," intimidating you into believing that you cannot possibly handle your own financial plan without them.

It is no big surprise that only 17 percent of Americans hire a financial advisor to help them with their financial planning. Why would they want to, when the message is, "It's a really hard and intimidating process, and that is why you need us. We don't care about you; we only really care about your money. It's up to you to figure out how to spend it; or not."

Some years ago, Cheryl had called me from the hospital to let me know that Jesse had become quite ill with a heart scare. For a while, they weren't sure what the outcome would be. Thankfully, he was stabilized, had bypass surgery, and is doing well now. At our next meeting, Cheryl expressed, "You were the first person we called after our son. I just want you to know, you feel like part of our family. Thank you for taking the time that you have with us over the years. I am not sure what we would have done without you."

I tell this story because before, I really had no idea how important it was to stay connected with my clients. How much more meaningful it is to continue to build and grow in our personal relationships. I have always said I am just merely the "Queen of Common Sense." But my life has been saved, too, by the love and appreciation I have received from people like Jesse and Cheryl. Without them, my "Why" is empty and without meaning. And, although it may sound like a cliché, I am thankful every day for the gifts I receive in knowing and helping the people I meet through my *work* life. This is my "Why."

CHAPTER 5

After sketching the faces, I begin to develop the character lines and shadows that expose the uniqueness of the individual. These details uncover a roadmap of past experiences, struggles, accomplishments, and expressions, as well as the frame of mind the person is in at that given time. These clues will often give me insights into how they cared for themselves, or if they smiled more than they frowned, or worried more than they played. If you look closely, these lines will tell the story of the impact their life experiences had on their overall well-being.

I try to see these same clues in the faces of my clients. What is worrying them? What is holding them back from doing what they really want to do? What have they succeeded in, and how can we bring those feelings of accomplishment to the surface? So many times, the good things get lost in all the worries that life brings. I try to bring the focus back around to the light—the "cans" versus the "cannots." I would much prefer seeing laugh lines versus worry lines on the faces of my clients and the people in the portraits I paint.

Do This First

Finding Your "Stuff"

FOR MANY, the thought of gathering thirty-five years of documents is daunting. Who really wants to do that? For some, it feels like pulling together generations of old photographs, trying to remember who these people are, then organizing them into endless albums. **The good news is that in our process, all you need to do is find your stuff, then we will take it from there.**

The Nuts and Bolts

Hopefully, you have already considered your "*Whys*" by taking time to run through the BFS Way Discovery Questionnaire exercise noted in Chapter 1. Our next step in the process is finding the *Nuts and Bolts*, the details of your present position. It's not as hard as it sounds.

We like to start with a guide of sorts, a checklist that will help you find what you need without leaving anything out. By using our BFS Document Checklist, you will know exactly what is pertinent to building an accurate financial plan. Later, when you're ready, it also provides a platform for you to upload copies of your information for us to review. You can find these on the Bonus page of our website at **BeckFS.com/Bonus.8.htm**

Try Our Way

Col. Parker came to us, thinking he had everything I needed to know right on his Excel spreadsheet. He resisted the idea that I would also want to review his original statements, as he had pages of data, complete with investment holdings, returns, and even a cash flow section. It was a beautiful document that must have taken him years to develop.

There was a problem, however. I had no proof that the numbers were accurate or up to date. The sheet was formatted in such a way that only he could decipher his formulas. I could not see how his accounts were titled or how much his employer was contributing. And I had no information on how much he was paying in taxes or what his deductions were. I could see he had a government pension coming in monthly, but was that figure before or after taxes? And, on an obscure page, I did find a list of credit cards, but no balances were listed.

I explained my dilemma to the colonel, and he finally relented and went online to review the BFS Document Checklist and uploaded the documents that were on the list. He called later and said that he had been surprised at how easy it was. His job was now done, and ours was just beginning.

I had belabored over asking Col. Parker to use our system. He was a man who was not used to being asked to do something differently. He was used to being in charge.

But in the end, I mustered up the courage to help him get in line with our system, and as it turned out, I am glad I did!

While organizing his information, we uncovered some profoundly serious concerns in his overall picture. The most daunting was the five credit card statements we were reviewing, which together had a total debt balance of $125,000. There was no hint of this on the spreadsheet. Was this the monster in *his* closet?

I fretted for days about how I would address this issue with him. How would I get him out of this debt? Would he listen? Would he be angry that it was even brought up since he never mentioned this to me before? I decided I had to do what I have always done: Build a debt-elimination plan, find a way out of the problem, and then show him the solution.

The other request I had made of Col. Parker was to complete the expenses section of our factfinder. He had completed much of it, and what he hadn't included, we were able to see when we linked all his bank accounts and credit card statements to his BFS Money Site. His spending items could then be uploaded and categorized, so we knew what his "Needs," "Wants," and "Desires" were.

More importantly, we found a cash flow surplus! And we needed that! He had been working in a career after retiring from the military and was making a good income. That, along with his pension, gave us some room to start working down the debts.

Turn your monster into a teddy bear.

I also needed to delicately explore with him how these debts originally came to be. He had tried to start his own business and had some enormous medical bills from an illness he previously had. While his insurance was excellent, he had tried some alternative remedies that were not covered. His health had returned, and he gave up his business, all of which told me that he was not a habitual spender. He had made some uninformed business moves and had some tough luck, but I knew he had what it took to eventually eliminate his debt.

If the Foundation Is Sound, the House Will Not Fall

What took Col. Parker an hour and a half to complete eventually saved him thousands of dollars. What he assumed at first was a big, unnecessary hassle became a lifesaving exercise in facing the realities that he needed to uncover. In the end, getting the correct data and working from a sound foundation made all the difference. His solutions were achievable, and he had the confidence that they were built on solid ground.

Even accomplished army colonels can struggle with fears and keep "monsters" hidden away. We all have fears and things we want to avoid. The problem is, the longer they're in the closet, the bigger they often get. And eventually, they will come out. In Col. Parker's case, he was now ready to take it on. He often reminds me that, as he puts it, "The best part was that you did all the work!" Not really. I would suggest that he did the hard part in letting everything come to light. I just organized it and showed him how he could make the undesirable parts go away.

The colonel is now fully debt-free and living a much more relaxed life. We had set a plan in action, found the cash flow surplus to make it happen, and he and his wife followed the roadmap exactly. Well, actually, *not* exactly. The debt-elimination program had been a five-year plan, which they reduced, on their own, to four years. The "monster" had been forced out of the closet, and now, as I kiddingly say, "The colonel has become the teddy bear."

CHAPTER 6

No two portraits are ever alike. No two eyes or ears, even on the same person, are ever the same. I must map out the detail individually. I cannot guess on the details by taking stock images from an art book. If I am off by just an eighth of an inch, the person I am trying to paint will never come into focus. Being detail-oriented can be a curse for some, but for me, it is a strength I am grateful for. If one has no patience for the facts, one's outcome will never turn out real.

The same is true when fine-tuning the details of a client's current situation. Attention to detail is what makes the plan work uniquely and exactly as it should within the context of the data. I have to prove those details to myself and not take for granted that what I am told is always the precise reality. To build confidence in my client's eyes, the details that support my recommendations must be "spot on."

Is It Time to Get Help?

Being a Good Saver Alone Is Not Enough

JANET WAS AN EXCELLENT SAVER, but she came close to losing half of her money. For years, she was the one who handled the money, who read the articles, who was planning for retirement. Kurt, her husband, really had no interest and was relieved that Janet "had it covered." When they came to me, they had just received her retirement plan statement and immediately saw they needed help.

Janet had met periodically with her plan representative, who gave her some "free advice" on where she might invest her funds, and she took it. By the time we met, her portfolio mirrored that of an aggressive twenty-something investor and not that of a sixty-six-year-old investor who was just forced into early retirement due to the COVID-19 pandemic.

"But I have done everything right," she tearfully expressed. She had faithfully saved the maximum amount allowable in her 401(k) for the last twenty years. She had run the retirement projections using a do-it-yourself website that confirmed she could retire successfully.

Recently she had asked her retirement plan representative if she could take some money out of her account to buy a new car, something she wanted to do before she retired. She had planned to pay the money back in six months when her CD came due. He had assured her that she could but never mentioned the possible pitfalls that could come along with it—the main one being that if she left the company before paying the money back, it would be classified as a withdrawal and be 100 percent taxable.

The other crisis was that it was early in the pandemic market cycle, and her portfolio had dropped over 25 percent in value. With no one to turn to, she panicked and moved all her remaining assets to cash. It took less than two months to severely impact a long-term strategy that had seemed to work for her before.

The Six Keys to a Financial Plan

There is so much that one can miss when trying to take on all the aspects of a financial plan. You may still be thinking, "I have done a fairly good job with saving over all these years; I think I can handle this. And I am not sure if paying an advisor is really worth it."

So, let me guide you through all that it takes to build a financial plan. To be effective, a plan must carefully work through and coordinate six key components. These components work together like pieces of a puzzle. If one is missing, the entire puzzle is not complete, and the plan doesn't work.

Finding Your Income

Starting with an income goal is undoubtedly the first step. However, so many will merely look at what they are currently earning and compare that to what they will bring in from Social Security and a pension, if they have one. Then, there is that arbitrary 4 percent withdrawal rate that they have been told is "safe" to take from their investments.

But what appears to be enough likely may not be.

What about inflation? How will your income be impacted by a 20 percent downfall in your investment portfolio? When is the best time to start taking your Social Security income? What survivor benefit pension option is best? Does the income goal include taxes, and from which "investment bucket" would be the best to take from first?

One of the most effective and risk-averse ways to set up an income plan is to time-segment it. This takes detailed tax assessment, investment allocation adjusting, and finally, logistics planning. These details should be coordinated by your team

Six Keys to a Financial Plan

- Cash Management & Income Needs

- Risk & Insurance

- Investment Management & Allocation Analysis

- Tax Management

- Financial Independence & Income Planning

- Estate & Legacy Planning

of qualified advisors. What *you* want to be focused on is seeing an automatic monthly check deposited into your checking account, on time, every time, and knowing the details behind the scenes are being taken care of.

Janet had not considered any of these things. If she had been able to see the impact that taking withdrawals would have on her retirement plan, she would most likely have recognized that she needed to back down on the risk she was taking in her portfolio. She also would have had a plan in place for when she did retire, which she had planned would take place in another year.

She also had better options available to her that she could have used to purchase a car. She was concerned about using her emergency reserves to pay for the car and did not want a car payment. As it turned out, she could have easily tapped into her cash or home equity line of credit for the short time that she needed. No one was there to help her consider all her options, and it cost her and her husband dearly.

Insurance for the "What-Ifs"
Often, those we work with own some form of life insurance. But many don't really understand the inner workings, and often,

it is temporary insurance that will not be in force when they die. Sadly, for most, the amount of life insurance originally purchased was based on what was affordable at the time. Rarely does the economic value of a person's earning power come into the equation, and it should.

Life insurance is meant to furnish the funds necessary to replace the income that was previously being provided by the mere fact that you were living. Think of yourself as a money-making machine. Whether the income comes from earnings, Social Security, or a pension, the key is to enable your loved ones to maintain their current standard of living after you die. So many believe that they no longer will need life insurance after they retire. However, I have found that *not* to be the case. There is almost always a negative financial impact when someone dies. Earnings cease, social security reduces, and pension benefits often stop or are reduced. And all these events typically happen after retirement, when many no longer have coverage.

It is not a matter of *if* one becomes uninsurable but rather, *when.* Janet had

life insurance that she thought she could keep after she retired. After reading an article about maximizing her pension plan, she had taken the irrevocable life-only pension benefit election. This meant that when she passed, her husband would no longer receive her pension benefits. They had planned for her insurance to make up the difference for her husband if she died first.

This plan can be highly effective. However, it should never be implemented using term insurance. Term insurance is temporary, and for this strategy to work effectively, it must include permanent insurance that will cover her through her lifetime, paying the benefit out no matter when she dies. If she lives a long life, likely her term insurance will no longer be in force, just when it is needed most. *This was not mentioned in the article.*

Janet quickly uncovered that her term insurance would drop when she no longer worked at the company, and to replace it would prove to be at an exorbitant cost. In addition, Janet had had cancer four years earlier and was currently not able to qualify

Think of Yourself as a Money-Making Machine

- If you die or become disabled prematurely, your retirement plan, as well as your income, will diminish greatly.

- If you die prematurely, even after retirement, your family's income will be reduced substantially.

- Insurance can keep your money-making machine working even if you can't.

for life insurance. Therefore, her husband would be forced to live with the risk of a reduced lifestyle if Janet passed first.

One other risk that had not been addressed was that of long-term care. I often say that **the single greatest risk to a lifetime portfolio is the possible cost of long-term care**. None of us want to think about it. Many don't want to plan for it, as then it feels as if we are saying it's OK to put us there. It's not, but sometimes it is required.

When teaching about this topic, I like to suggest that a person picture their spouse as the one in the nursing home. It's cold, I know, but it then brings to light what

the "community spouse" might be facing. With an additional income draw of over $80,000 per year (in today's dollars), the person at home could be faced with living their life very differently. Certainly, the Go-Go Years have ended, but the spouse at home still needs to pay the utility bills and buy food.

According to the Indiana Long Term Care Partnership Program, seven out of ten individuals will need home health-care and/or nursing home care sometime during their lives, and currently, 40 percent of those using long-term care services in the US are between the ages of eighteen and sixty-four. **Overall, individ-**

uals living over the age of sixty-five will have a 60-70 percent chance of needing some type of long-term care service.[4] So, the risk is real, and solutions must be considered if the cost is more than your portfolio can sustain.

Finding Your Volatility Comfort Zone

Diversifying your portfolio based on asset classes alone is not enough. In these times, it is a two-dimensional attempt to reduce risk. In today's world, information literally flies through the airways, some of which is accurate, much of which is not. Making financial decisions based on news and articles alone is very–let me repeat *very*–risky.

Janet thought she had it covered. She felt positive about the market, and all the information she read supported that optimism. But life is full of curveballs, and the COVID-19 pandemic was a big one. It was undiscovered territory; there had been nothing like it in our lifetimes, and she was scared.

Most of my money-management partners were nervous too. We would talk two or three times per day during that period. But what we all found was that the fundamentals were still there. The panic peddlers didn't seem to have the facts behind them, and the federal government was pouring stimulus money into the economy at unprecedented levels.

Our managers held steady, looking for companies that would bode well in the new normal of the pandemic. They depended on their long-standing research teams, focusing on the fundamentals and underlying health of the individual companies they had our clients' portfolios invested in.

Our portfolios were *not* index funds. Just consider the S&P 500 Index, which became highly overweighted in what Jim Cramer, the television host of CNBC's *Mad Money*, named the "FAANG" stocks: Facebook, Amazon, Apple, Netflix, and Google. No sound investment strategy would have ever allowed a portfolio to be so overweighted in just a few stocks, due to the added risk associated with that imbalance.

Index funds do one thing: They mirror the holdings in indexes. Yes, they are cheap, and that is because there is no perspective around risk and return and no management having anything to do with your own risk tolerance or income goals.

In the bond sectors, our clients benefited from not having their bond positions held in mutual funds. Most were invested in individual bonds allowing our portfolio managers to hold them to maturity, unlike mutual fund managers who had to sell their bonds, often at untimely intervals, to raise the cash necessary to pay nervous investors who were pulling out of their funds.

Our portfolios were strategically designed to weather these storms, and it was my job to communicate this to my clients. I knew I had explored each family's own risk tolerance in detail, and times like these would uncover whether I had succeeded in finding their pain points.

I also knew that the mix of securities in each portfolio was thought out in detail and customized for each family I served. I had chosen conservative money managers who had many years of success and expe-

rience. And we knew that our time-segmenting process insulated our income portfolios against market downturns by preventing the need to sell securities at a loss to fund the current income requirements of our clients.

Prior to working with our team, Janet hadn't had access to the research being done behind the scenes regarding her portfolio. No one was looking out for her own life goals, and more importantly, her risk tolerance. And no one was there to talk to her when things got rough. Sometimes the most important component is just having someone, a professional, to hold your hand while things are uncertain. Financial articles and news shows won't provide that. In fact, they add to the fear.

Living on What You Have Saved—for Life
One of the biggest fears many have is running out of money before we die. It can be a paralyzing fear, one that takes away our confidence to spend our money on the things we want. While everything must be within reason, it is often more doable than we might think.

Saving is not investing, and thus keeping all of our money "safe" in a checking or savings account will not provide the income we want. But on the flip side, putting your money out there in the market where it can go up and down is terrifying as well.

Janet had those fears and therefore had almost as much money in cash at her bank as she had in her 401(k) plan. This was helpful in finding ways to make up for some of the pitfalls that had recently made their financial independence look shaky.

I knew that Janet and Kurt's risk tolerance was extremely low. I also knew it would be very risky to keep them invested as aggressively as they had been in the past to try and earn back what they had lost. We decided to work from their new starting point but find solutions that they could live with in all economic times.

To handle Janet's retirement funds, I introduced them to a money-management team that focused on building customized income portfolios. We held at least three years of Janet and Kurt's income needs in cash and short-term bonds so that they would not be taking withdrawals from securities that could be fluctuating in the market.

We also found a solution for some of their cash that still afforded them a guarantee of principal, which was especially important to Janet. This solution also provided a guaranteed lifetime income component that would help with the loss of pension income that Kurt would experience if Janet passed away first. The income was guaranteed to pay out until the end of both of their lives and would even double if they needed long-term nursing care.

Additionally, we considered their Social Security timing options. Kurt was younger than Janet and had been self-employed for many years. It made sense for Kurt to start taking his Social Security funds earlier and then shift over to Janet's when she started taking hers at age seventy. By waiting, Janet's benefit amount increased to 132 percent of her full retirement age amount, and that would be helpful in providing the income they felt they lost due to the reduction in Janet's retirement account.

Albert Einstein once said, "The hardest thing in the world to understand is income taxes." It's best to get help from a professional.

- Take advantage of all income-tax deductions and strategies.

- Be aware of changes in the estate tax laws that may be coming.

- Know all the ramifications of the actions you plan to take *before* taking them.

Keeping Uncle Sam in Tow

We live in the greatest country in the world, and our taxes help maintain our quality of life. However, many tax laws that differ throughout our states can be detrimental to our lifetime savings. It is important to understand the ever-changing laws that apply not only to income taxes but also property, capital gains, and estate tax. Being up to date with these latest rules can work in your favor. Or, if you are not up to date, they will surely work against you.

Janet did not have good direction when she decided to take a loan out of her 401(k). She hadn't planned on a forced retirement due to circumstances out of her control. She may have made a different decision had she been informed of all her possible solutions before taking that one action. She most likely knew there were other choices but didn't have anyone she could discuss them with. In the end, she made the choice because it was easy; she could just log into her 401(k) and complete the loan request form online.

We couldn't do anything to change the tax impact that happened because of the 401(k) withdrawal, but we could reduce her income taxes going forward. We placed her cash in a tax-deferred account where the interest would only be taxable at the time she started taking withdrawals. In the meantime, her interest would be reinvested, and no taxes would be due.

Leaving an Orderly Estate

Planning for what we want to have happen when we die is just no fun. First, we have to admit that we are not going to get out of this alive, and then we need to think through the ramifications of each decision that we make. It is a hard step, but one that must be done for everything to work together.

We think of estate planning as planning for our death. But first, we must plan for the "what if's" of still being alive. What if we are incapacitated for a time but still need someone to handle our affairs? What if there are bills to be paid or money transfers to be made? What if there are lifesaving decisions to be made on our behalf? These are all things that need to be addressed— and with someone we trust.

We then can consider the best and least expensive ways to plan for the estate to pass to our heirs. There are reasons to have trusts and not to have trusts. There are different types of trusts that are set up for specifically different reasons. It may be important to avoid the costs and additional time that probate incurs, especially if you own property in more than one state. **Some of our estate-planning wishes can be accomplished just by titling our assets in a certain way and specifying our beneficiaries correctly.**

Janet and Kurt had a will, a living will, and a durable power of attorney in place. They also had a living trust. At first glance, their estate documents appeared to be in good order. But additional digging revealed that the trust would not carry out any of the actions that they had desired because no assets were set up to pass through it. For this trust to work, assets, such as their house and bank accounts, needed to be re-titled *to the trust*. The beneficiary designations in their life insurance policies needed to be updated as well.

As is often the case, the attorney did a fine job with the actual documents but did not provide clear instructions for Janet and Kurt. There was no coordinated effort or follow-up to verify that they had re-titled assets as needed to fund the trust. In addition, they had not changed their beneficiaries so that the appropriate funds would pass through their trust as they intended, rather than going directly to their heirs.

The Cost of Not Having an Advisor

The actions that Janet and Kurt took without the guidance of an advisor were expensive.

- Taking a $40K loan from her 401(k). **Cost: $12K** in taxes

- Losing life insurance to fund survivor pension, causing Kurt to lose $1,300 monthly for the rest of his life if Janet passes first. **Cost: $234K** if he lives fifteen years after Janet passes.

- Selling all 401(k) holdings at the bottom of a market cycle. **Cost: $150K**

- Not having a contingency plan for long-term care costs. **Possible Cost: $247,350 (**National average cost of nursing home care semiprivate room,

$255/day[5], average stay = 485 days[6], multiplied by two = 970 days)

The Benefits of Having an Advisor

- Timed the Social Security withdrawals to increase their monthly income by 32 percent.

- Fully strategized an income plan for uninterrupted income, even in times of market downturns.

- Provided some risk protection from long-term care expenses.

- Increased the return and decreased taxes on cash assets.

- Found a new guaranteed income solution to replace the lost pension benefit for Kurt.

- Completed the final steps needed to allow the estate documents to work as intended.

CHAPTER 7

When choosing a subject I want to paint, I need to first decide what it is I want to say. What message or tone or even question do I want to pose within the context of the composition? Sometimes I just want the image to be someone that others would like to sit next to on a park bench and talk with. Or maybe they'd find something in that person that they would like to emulate if they had the opportunity.

When sitting in my conference room, I often hear comments such as, "I wish I had done what she had." Or "I really don't have what he has, and therefore I could never do that." This often comes from just not getting the encouragement to explore their true abilities.

I often give a ukulele as a gift to clients who have just experienced a life-changing event such as retirement or the loss of a loved one. These are big changes in identity, and I want my message always to be, "You can do this." You can be the bright-eyed, inspiring lady sitting on the park bench or the fun-loving man strumming a ukulele. You can be anyone you want to be—and even someone you never thought you could be.

What's Missing in Your Financial Plan?

You Just Never Know When ...

AFTER DRIVING FOR THREE HOURS through southern Indiana, I turned onto a long, winding dirt road that eventually came to a small rustic farmhouse in dire need of fresh paint. Three dogs were barking at my tires and running out of the house were more children than I could count. As always when I encountered dogs, I opened my car door and talked to them while gathering my briefcase, careful not to look at them directly until they had time to smell my scent and decide I was OK.

As I stepped out of my car, the children gathered and chattered all around, excited with the prospect of having a visitor—something I don't think they had had for quite some time. I looked at the front of the house. Standing on the doorstep, holding an infant, was a beautiful woman with long blond hair. She wore a cotton skirt and sleeveless blouse, most likely hand-me-downs from some other time period. That was the first time I met Sharon.

Through all the frenzy of the dogs and delightful children, she invited me into her kitchen that looked like it was right out of the '50s. The worn linoleum floor was a greenish turquoise, and the wooden table was covered with an embroidered table-cloth. The fan in the window blessed us with a welcome breeze from the hot summer air.

There we sat, each staring at the other in amazement. She was in her element, children swirling in and out, her steadfast attention never leaving my gaze. I, meanwhile, wore my "dress for success" attire, complete with pump shoes and a smart briefcase. I just couldn't take my eyes off her. She truly was the most beautiful woman I had ever seen.

I found out years later that she had thought the same about me. We were close in age, both in our early thirties at the time, but had chosen such different paths in our lives. In the years that followed, I would find reasons to drive the three hours just to have the opportunity to sit with her in her kitchen, have some tea, and talk. She would ask me to tell her about everything I did in my life, and I would ask her to do the same. We studied each other, we listened intently to the other and, in the end, became lasting friends.

Sharon's husband was a farmer and a man of few words. He would come in during lunchtime, and Sharon would fix him something to eat. It was then that I talked with them about their need for life insurance, and they listened. James was not one to spend a lot of time on the details, but he loved his family and signed the paperwork, stating that $50 per month was all they could afford.

I knew they needed as much life insurance as the $50 would pay for. Looking around at all of the deferred maintenance in their little home, I frankly was amazed he agreed to use any of their hard-earned funds on insurance. We wrote a $500K, twenty-year, term-life policy on him, as that would provide the most amount of insurance for the least amount of cost. In their case, the death benefit was paramount.

Little did I know how true that would become. Two years later, I received a call from Sharon. Tom had been killed in a farm accident earlier that day. I was dumbfounded. I couldn't get in my car fast enough. The three-hour drive seemed like six that night.

It was then that I realized the impact I could make on the people's lives that I helped plan for. Sharon was terribly shaken up, but when we went through her finances a few weeks later, it was such a relief knowing that, financially, she was going to be OK. $500K was not a lot of money, but she was able to pay off the farm loan, invest a portion of the funds for her own retirement, and purchase life insurance on herself, for the unlikely possibility that she would not live to raise her nine children to adulthood.

I helped Sharon find an accountant to assist her with the bookkeeping, and she found a farmer to rent her farm. This, along with the Social Security benefits, provided enough income for them to live comfortably and remain in their own home. In the years that followed, we even found enough in her budget to make improvements on her little house, and the family fared well.

On one of our visits, I mentioned to Sharon that she really needed to have a will drafted and to designate a guardian for her children. I had met Sharon's mother twice. She was an overpowering, controlling person, and I knew Sharon would not want her to raise her children. And I knew just enough about estate planning to know that most likely, if something ever happened to Sharon, her mother would be the court's likely candidate.

Together we found an estate planning attorney who drafted the important documents. Sharon appointed her sister as guardian and set up a trust that would be funded by the life insurance that we had put in place some years earlier. That trust would provide the guidance and the funds her sister and brother-in-law would require to raise their nieces and nephews in the unlikely event that she passed away early in her life.

And once again, little did we know how important those documents were. One afternoon, Sharon had severe stomach pain. She was rushed to the hospital where, after many tests, they decided to do some exploratory surgery. Finding a large tumor in her abdomen, the doctors knew there was nothing they could do. She had stage four stomach cancer. Three months later, Sharon was gone.

My heart was broken. We had always talked about how we would grow old together and watch how each of our lives would turn out. This was not supposed to happen. It never is.

I was so thankful, however, for the time I had been given with Sharon, and I knew that the planning we did for her children was going to pay off. They were now orphans, all nine of them. But due to the acts of love she did for her family, they would be well cared for. Sharon's sister and brother-in-law would raise the children,

Leaving an orderly estate is one of the final acts of love you can bestow on the ones you love.

- When was the last time you updated your will?

- Do you have a current durable power of attorney and living will?

- If you have minor children, have you appointed a legal guardian?

- Do you own property in two different states? Have you thought of the ramifications of putting your heirs through two probates?

- Do you own a business, and if so, do you have a succession plan in place?

- Do you have a system that will enable your heirs to find your important documents?

which would not be an easy feat. It helped that they knew they would have the funds necessary to take on the enormous task.

Today, over thirty years later, I still think of Sharon often. Her children are all thriving adults, many married and with children of their own. I don't make the drive to her hometown as often as I used to, as the family is now spread out and living in towns all over the country. Two of her children, however, still live on the farm, a fact that brings me great comfort when driving by the still inviting, long and winding, dirt road.

Why a CFP® Professional?

Not long after Sharon passed, I became a CERTIFIED FINANCIAL PLANNER™ (CFP®) professional. I often say that it was the single greatest gift I ever gave to myself in my career. While I had been assisting clients for over twelve years, at that time, there were areas in which I just didn't have the confidence to help them. I would research to find what they needed in a particular situation, but I knew I needed more.

The role of the financial planner, I soon discovered, is not to do it all but rather to be the coordinator. I learned that I needed to have extensive knowledge in all the components that makes up a complete financial plan, but equally important, I needed to find and thoroughly vet the experts to help implement the plan.

Today we call our team the "Under-One-Roof Planning Team." Together, under my direction, we coordinate a plan with all of the advisors one might need to be sure the work is complete and integrated with the total financial planning vision. And the key is that they all need to work together to implement the plan. A complete Under-One-Roof Planning Team would consist of:

• A Tax Advisor

• An Estate Law Attorney

• A Personalized Wealth & Portfolio Manager

• An Insurance Professional

• A Bank Professional/ Loan Officer

Not having this team in place is like having a specialist doctor who writes a prescription for only one condition. If all the other doctors don't know the overall condition of the patient, including the mix of medications he or she is taking, things could be missed, which could produce unwanted side effects, and at worst, a disastrous outcome.

We saw what could happen when things are not coordinated. Also, we have seen what can happen when the team comes together for the greater good of the client. In Sharon's case, we found an excellent CPA and attorney who helped us complete all the components of her financial plan. It was my job to be sure there was nothing missing or left out and that if something did happen, the plan would work as smoothly as possible. For Sharon, it was sadly the last real act of love she was able to do for her family.

We also saw in Kurt and Janet's case what lack of coordination could potentially do to what appeared to otherwise be a well-thought-out plan. A plan is not just the completion of a few separate acts; it must have the coordination and the experts behind it to enable it to work effectively.

What Sets a CFP® Professional Apart?

Many people think all "financial advisors" are *certified*, but that is just not the case. When you hire a CFP® professional, you are working with an advisor who has met rigorous qualifications for financial planning and has demonstrated the knowledge required to deliver a holistic financial plan. As part of the certification, they commit to high ethical standards and must acquire several years of experience before they can call themselves CFP® professionals. To maintain their certification, they must also complete continuing education requirements so that they remain up to date with the latest components in financial planning.

What Is a Fiduciary, and Why Is That Important?

Most importantly, CFP® professionals have made a commitment to the CFP® Board to act in your best interests. A fiduciary is someone who will put your interests ahead of his or her own. This is important because, in some situations, the interests of a financial advisor may conflict with your own interests. A fiduciary has an obligation to disclose the conflicts of interest and continue to put your interests first. This may seem like common sense, but not all financial professionals have a fiduciary obligation.

What Questions Should I Ask?

When first meeting people, I often find that they are not quite sure how to go about interviewing a potential advisor to help them with their planning. I would suggest that there are ten basic questions that should be answered to your satisfaction while assessing an advisor candidate. They are:

THE ART OF THE PLAN

1. What Are Your Credentials?

Obviously, I am partial to working with a CFP® professional for the reasons I noted above. But it is also helpful to understand what other licenses your advisor candidate holds. For instance, in addition to being a CFP® professional, I hold a FINRA Series 6, 7, 63, and SIE license, as well as Life and Health licenses in numerous states. I am also registered as an Investment Advisor Representative.

2. Will You Have a Fiduciary Duty to Me?

As mentioned, a CFP® professional is bound to work at all times as a fiduciary, putting your needs before their own. Even if your advisor candidate is not a CFP® professional, you will want to ask if they are an Investment Advisory Representative, as they, too, are bound by the duty of acting as a fiduciary. In addition, you may want to ask if they have any conflicts of interest that could impact their advice.

3. What Services Do You Offer?

There are many different services an advisor can offer. Some may also have other designations such as CPA or ChFC, etc. They may provide insurance services in-house and may be certified to write their state's long-term care plans. It is good to know just what services you might be able to utilize, along with the financial planning assistance you are seeking.

4. What Types of Clients Do You Typically Work With?

It is always a good idea to inquire about the advisor candidate's typical client and whether they are similar to you. What are their clients' typical age group and needs? What are the advisor's specialties, and are they in tune with your needs?

For instance, my firm's expertise is primarily in providing financial planning for families and small businesses. The average age of our clients is fifty-five to seventy-five; however, we are now beginning to work with many of our clients' second and third generations. Therefore, we do not limit our services to just one demographic. Many of our mature clients are in the retirement stage of their planning, which requires extensive focus on income and estate planning.

Our average clients have invested assets of $1M to $5M and an average net worth of $3M to $10M. These averages reflect the fact that many of our clients have worked with us for many years and began the process with a much lower net worth.

Requiring a minimum investment requirement directly opposes our belief that every person should have the opportunity to fulfill their own personal life purpose. Everyone has to start somewhere and getting people to their ideal financial destination securely and with their "Why" in mind is what we do best.

5. What Are Your Fees, and How Are You Paid?

"Will I be asked to buy something?" might be your first thought. Finding out how an advisor gets paid can be confusing. There are really three basic ways an advisor can get paid for the services they offer.

Fee-Based

The first would be fee-based, meaning that the advisor will get paid a fee for the advice and services they provide you. This could be an ongoing subscription fee or a one-time fee. It could be based on an hourly rate or a flat fee for specific services. There could also be ongoing fees for the management of your investments, which are typically between 1 and 3 percent. Some advisors don't charge planning fees if you allow them to manage your investments, typically with a certain minimum in mind.

Commission-Based

An advisor can also earn income through commissions paid by the various product vendors. Many of the solutions provided are necessary to build a successful financial plan. These may include life, health, and annuity companies, as well as long-term care insurance.

Some advisors earn commissions when providing certain class shares of mutual funds and/or when servicing brokerage accounts, which at times could prove to be the most suitable in a given situation.

Fee- and Commission-Based

This form of payment, which is more of a hybrid approach, is the model I have chosen for Beck Financial Strategies. This payment method allows the advisor and you to be flexible with the planning services you require.

For instance, you may only be seeking financial planning advice for a one-time fee. Or you may need ongoing guidance that might include a subscription service to a financial planning website. You may also find that managing your own investments is not your expertise, and you are looking for an advisor to manage those for you. And last, you may need some insurance or some other financial instruments that can be purchased from your advisor.

There is nothing wrong with any of these solutions, as long as you are aware of how your advisor is paid and feel that the payment is appropriate for your unique situation.

6. Are You the Only Advisor I Will Be Working With?

Most firms will have an administrative team to assist in gathering your information, setting up meetings, and even meeting with you directly in addition to meeting with your advisor. Some firms may find that a junior advisor might be more suitable and affordable if your plan is of a simpler nature.

At our firm, we encourage you to get to know all of the members of our staff and our Under-One-Roof Planning Team. We have fully licensed team members that offer prompt, accurate assistance to our clients daily. The financial planning consultations, however, typically start with me. I believe accessibility must be first and foremost to your experiencing a beneficial relationship with your advisor, and thus our "open door policy" has always been our #1 priority.

You may also be introduced to a member of our Under-One-Roof Planning Team of professionals if you need other services that we cannot offer directly, such as Medicare and estate planning or tax services. These are independent advisors whom you would hire independently of our firm. You may choose to enlist in their services or use your own advisors outside of our firm. That is totally up to you.

7. What If I Move from One Advisor to Another?

After you have worked with your new advisor, if you decide you want to move your investments or change a relationship you had with a previous advisor, you may need to know certain things. For instance, you may want to ask what the costs would be, if any? Do you have to call the advisor and instigate these changes, or will the new advisor do this for you? What are the benefits and disadvantages?

You want to be clear on these points if you decide at some point that you want to make a change. This may be premature in the first interview, but it is worthy of considering how the advisor candidate might answer these questions.

8. What If I Move to Another State?

In these times, especially in the COVID-19 era, you can work with a financial advisor really from anywhere. Zoom and other forms of virtual meeting platforms have made connecting much easier, and the experience can still be highly effective and informative.

We provide financial planning services for clients all over the country. As long as your advisor is licensed and registered in the state where you live, they can continue to provide the services that you need. If our clients move to a state that we are not currently registered in, we promptly get registered in that state so that there is no break in the planning experience. Some advisors at other companies may choose not to work in other states, so that is something you should keep in mind if you plan on moving or on living part-time in other locations.

9. What If Something Happens to You?

Interestingly enough, many advisors don't have their own estate and succession plans in order. Financial advisors become disabled and die too, and there must be a plan in place if that were to happen.

I have always had a written succession plan in place, complete with an appointed successor advisor. Along with our licensed and seasoned team members, who know our clients extensively, we have a written policy in place that is designed to make an unexpected transition as smooth and comfortable as possible. In addition, we have an exceptional group of business partners who are committed to assisting our team and you with continued, uninterrupted financial planning services if such an event should ever happen.

10. Have You Ever Been Publicly Disciplined?

You will also want to ask your advisor candidate if he/she has ever been publicly disciplined by any organization that oversees his or her conduct. This discipline could be for any unlawful or unethical actions. Information about financial advisors who are subject to Financial Industry Regulatory Authority or Securities and Exchange Commission oversight is available through FINRA's BrokerCheck, **https://brokercheck.finra.org**, and the SEC's Investment Adviser Public Disclosure databases, **https://adviserinfo.sec.gov.**

Information also is available on the websites for the state securities or insurance regulator in the states in which a CFP® professional is licensed for securities or insurance. As a nonprofit professional body, the CFP® Board has its own process for enforcing its standards. CFP® Board disciplinary history of a CFP® professional can be found through the Verify tool. **https://www.cfp.net/verify-a-cfp-professional**

You can research information about me on the links below.

https://brokercheck.finra.org/individual/summary/1399902
https://adviserinfo.sec.gov/individual/summary/1399902
https://www.cfp.net/verify-a-cfp-professional/
results?limit=20&pg=1&lastName=Beck&firstName=Nancy&state=in

In a Nutshell

If you are hesitating, ask yourself, "What is missing?"

It is important that we don't make this more complicated than it needs to be. To learn more, you have to take that first step to talk to someone. After you feel you have done your vetting and have decided to move forward with a plan, we have an easy process that assures that your plan will be comprehensive, specific to you, with the peace of mind that nothing will be missed.

We first want to solve the Strategy steps:

- Understanding your vision for the future.

- Getting the actual data and copies of statements.

- Reviewing all documents to be sure they coordinate with your wishes.

Then it's our turn to provide you with the Planning steps:

- Giving you the real picture today and the solutions to make it better for tomorrow.

- Providing the BFS Money Site tool to assist you in continuing to keep your information at hand, up to date, and coordinated for you and your family.

- Keeping your plan current with any changes in laws that could affect or change your intended outcome.

All you need to do is get us the data and any signed information and sharing agreements that may be required for our Under-One-Roof Planning Team or your own advisor team. Then it's up to us to get you the answers you need to start living your life confidently.

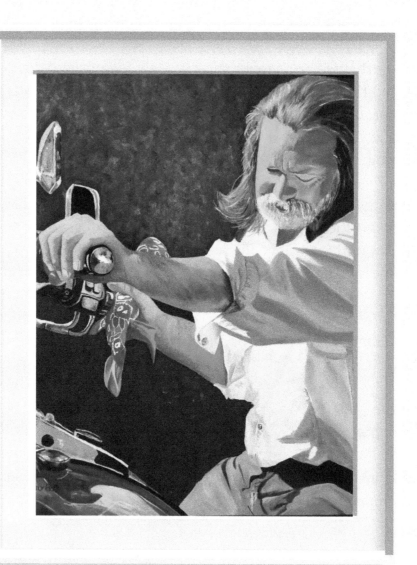

CHAPTER 8

Finding the correct color is essential to painting a pleasing portrait. This component of art takes practice. Mixing color does not come naturally at first, and in the early days, I used a color wheel to be sure that the hue I wanted didn't eventually turn into mud.

As I have grown in the craft, I have found that mixing less and using "cleaner" colors, in layers, gives a unique dimension to the painting. I paint the elements I want most in focus with more layers and thicker paint while using thinner, more greyed-out color to smooth the details that aren't so important. I have learned that things farther away will appear bluer, and things in sunlight will require more yellow. All this just comes with experience.

My experience with building financial plans has evolved over the years as well. My techniques continue to advance, and the tools we use have improved substantially—yet also have become more complex. I find, as in painting, that to be truly effective, I need to stay with it, continuing to learn new techniques and research new solutions that will help my clients achieve the outcomes they are striving for. And as importantly, I need to bring the most meaningful components to the forefront, so they are clear and easily visualized.

Getting On with Your Life

Good Problems to Have

IT'S SO FUNNY to see clients come in after working with us for a while, now contemplating a whole new set of problems—nice problems, but new questions all the same.

Sandy and Tom felt they would be financially secure, as they really hadn't been spending any of their savings. But with the new financial plan came new enlightenments. They would never spend all that they had in their lifetime, so now, the question was: What should they do with some of the funds?

The possibilities were real, but they just didn't have any idea how to think about their money differently. They understood they could spend more on themselves, but they had what they needed and were happy with their existing lifestyle.

They were continually active with their church and had four grandchildren that they liked to help in some way. Their original plan was to leave their estate to their heirs and some to the church, if there was anything left to leave. But now, they could enjoy doing some gifting while they were alive to enjoy it.

We brought in the attorney and set up a lifetime gifting program that would be set on autopilot unless they decided to change it. We transferred funds directly from their IRA to their church, avoiding income taxes while providing funds for causes they were passionate about. We also placed their second home inside a trust so that probate would not be an issue for their heirs.

In addition, we took a hard look at their investment portfolio. After retiring, they had left their investments in their old retirement plans because they knew how to log in and view those accounts. They *knew* this company; they had used them for years. They were comfortable, and they were also certain their fees were less.

But what we uncovered was that many of the fees were hidden, and the funds were merely index funds, following the holdings that the underlying indexes reflected. This portfolio had nothing to do with Tom and Sandy's risk tolerance or personal beliefs. In fact, they were actually against some of the underlying holdings due to their particular convictions, but they had no choice in the matter. And very importantly, they had no real hands-on management around their own tolerance for market swings compared to the volatility their current portfolio exposed them to.

With their level of net worth, I encouraged them to consider having a coordinated portfolio designed just for them. They would own individual stocks and bonds when possible and would be able to exclude any that were not in line with their personal standards. They also had

"all of their eggs in one basket," with their non-retirement accounts invested in the same fashion with the same fund family as well.

In the end, after careful comparisons, yes, the fees in their current portfolio were less, but not by much. And they had no access to the people managing their funds, no individualized tax planning, and no real picture of what they owned in the way of the underlying securities. They could see a report that revealed how their accounts were broken up between equities, bonds, and cash, but not much else. **They decided the extra fee was well worth the added value of Active Management designed specifically for their family's needs.**

Sandy and Tom's life became filled with less worry and more confidence, knowing that their overall financial picture was exactly in tune with their wishes. Holidays were more meaningful as they were able to see in real life what their grandchildren did with the gifts they were given. With some guidance, their grandchildren learned to invest some, save some, and spend some on meaningful things that would make them think of Grammy and Gramps. The plan had just evolved to a new stage, and it was more about feeding their souls than their bank accounts.

Don't Wish You Had Done It Sooner

Often, people can move from a current life position to an aspired way of life more quickly than they might think. In one of our reviews with Cindy and Mark, they mentioned that such had been the case with them. They had made a lot of changes to get to the place they wanted to be. They loved cruising, so they consciously moved to a town in Florida near cruise ship ports. They planned six or seven cruises per year and were enjoying their lives immensely. They both had worked for the federal government and had good income sources and more than sufficient funds to get them through their retirement years.

During one of our reviews, as we went through their BFS Money Site, they mentioned one regret they had about their plan. "We love our new life," Mark expressed, "but I wish we had done this sooner. We just had no idea that we really could live this way."

Let Your Advisor Do the Work

I hear regrets like Mark's more often than I'd like to admit. Is it time for you to really consider all of your options with the time you have left? Could it be that new opportunities are just around the corner? Might you be able to do some of the things you've dreamed of sooner than you thought? Maybe yes, and maybe not yet—but with a plan, you'll most definitely get there sooner.

Many times, creating a financial plan is one thing, but the idea of keeping it up is another. Often, that is the one roadblock that holds people back from taking the initial action of building a plan. It seems at first that it's going to be a lot of work keeping a financial plan current. But once you know the process, you can lay those concerns to rest.

For our clients, keeping up with their financial picture is important, and they

find their BFS Money Site to be a key component to their day-to-day money management. It is so easy for them to log into one place to see, in real-time, how things look. They can contact me with a question about a particular account, knowing that I can view the account details as well, which leads to quick answers and meaningful discussions without a lot of prep time.

The management of keeping your financial plan current and relevant can be an easy process as well. The BFS Money Site is one tool, but touching base at least annually is important as well. Our Annual Review process takes truly little of your precious time but allows us to continue to be in touch with your situation and your changing wish list. We also research things for you, such as the changes in the economic environment, new tax laws, and any other current events that may impact your financial plan. When we meet for your review, we will be ready to discuss any recommended changes so you can make informed decisions quickly and easily as they come up.

If it can be that simple, don't you think it may be time to start planning, and then living, your ideal life?

You're just one step away from
a new and improved life.

PART 3

NOW FOR THE "GO-GO YEARS"

"Happiness is not something ready-made. It comes from your own actions."
—The Dalai Lama

CHAPTER 9

The most difficult stage of my painting process is that of working in the background. This, at times, will take months, leaving the character to sit on the easel, surrounded by the bright red-orange underpainting, waiting patiently for me to figure out what direction to take. They have to be somewhere that they would enjoy, that they would fit in. The light must be coming from the same direction as the light that is reflected on the rest of their image. It all just has to fit together as if there was never any question; this is where they need to be.

The same is true for me when presenting a financial plan. I often ask myself, "Will I be able to give them confidence that they can afford the life they want? Have I missed something important that will throw the entire plan off track?"

The good news is that, unlike a finished painting, a financial plan is always evolving, and edits can easily be made along the way, keeping it relevant to the current situation.

CHAPTER 9

What Really Matters to You?

From Dream to Reality

YOU MIGHT THINK this book is about planning for retirement. It's not. It is about planning for your ideal life at whatever age you are. My hope is that my words will bring you closer to the idea that we are given only so much time, and if you want to make changes in your life, there is no time like the present to do so.

We often cling to our own misguided beliefs that we will do things differently once we retire. But the fact is, there is no good reason not to start making those changes now. Even if you are not financially ready to stop working entirely, I would still encourage you to start living your best life today. Yes, today—as soon as you are finished reading this book!

Change is hard. Being afraid of change can be paralyzing, and thus it is easier to use work as an excuse for the things you chose not to make a priority in your life. Priorities won't magically change once

Don't fear that your life will end. Fear that it will never begin.

you're retired. **If you are not making changes while you are working, you most likely won't have a vastly different life once you're retired.**

If you want a better marriage, or a more meaningful relationship with a family member, start now. If you want to learn a new hobby, to start exercising, or to pick up an old instrument you played in college, start now. If you want to travel more or find some new, more interesting friends, start now. Once you become more dynamic, so too will the world around you.

FEAR is "False Evidence Appearing Real." INTENTION is the power to move through fear. What you are thinking most often determines what happens in your future. **Don't be afraid that your life will end; be afraid that it will never begin.** If you think you can, you will. If you think you can't, you won't.

Questions to Ask Yourself

Ask yourself these simple questions.

What would you like to do more of?

- _____

- _____

- _____

What would you like to do less of?

- _____

- _____

- _____

If you could achieve these wishes, how would that make you feel?

_____

_____

What would these wishes allow you to do or achieve?

_____

_____

The Graveyard Is Full of Irreplaceable People

I have posed these questions to many of our clients and to some of the guests seated at our Key West dinner table. In the beginning of their journey, many were shy and timid and not very certain about their answers.

Carole had mentioned many times that she just couldn't retire yet. The time wasn't right. There were too many people depending on her at her high-stress job, and there was really no one to take her place.

Then COVID-19 came to town and hit Carole extremely hard. She collapsed in the parking lot while going into work and was rushed to the hospital. She was one of the first to contract the virus, and the treatments were still very experimental. She remained in the ICU for sixteen days, most of those days lying on her stomach to keep her lungs from filling with fluid. She was fighting for her life, and she had a lot of time to reflect.

Carole told herself that if she survived this, she would live her life differently. She had things she still wanted to do. Her time became her most important concern, and she concluded that she had to change her life—now.

And change her life she did. After her recovery, she helped her employer find a replacement and then retired two months later. "Graveyards," she often says, "are full of irreplaceable people; I didn't want to be one of them."

We had been working on Carole and Alan's financial plan for many years and had assured them that financial independence was attainable. We were just waiting for Carole to give herself permission to retire along with her husband.

She had always traveled to Key West for vacations, but she and Alan looked at their cash flow and found renting was just as expensive as buying. And so, they decided to purchase a condo in the southernmost town they both loved and named it their "Time Together Townhouse."

Carole is busier now than ever, doing things of her choosing. She has never been healthier and has started playing, of all things, the ukulele. She counsels fellow parishioners in her church and has found true meaning in her life.

One evening in Key West, she brought a guest to our dinner table who recently retired and seemed lost in her next phase of life. Carole, always providing the most spot-on advice, assured her, "Be patient; it will come." The rest of us at the table quietly smiled in the candlelight and nodded our heads. Sam, however, could not hold his excitement. "Yes," he blurted, "but you have to be open to it. And when you are, you'll never go back!"

The Facts Are Real

Beyond the enticing emotion of living your ideal life, there are facts that cannot be disputed when developing a well-thought-out financial plan designed around you.

Fact #1 Your Opportunity Is Real!

Just consider how different Janet and Kurt's life would have been had they not sought some financial planning advice. We learned what their costs were for not getting help sooner. But we also found that with some individualized planning, they were able to redirect the path they were on by implementing solutions that brought them back to being financially sound. And they did that before it was too late.

Without our "intervention," Wayne would never have started stepping away from his computer and stopped worrying about his money. He would have never seen that *his time* was the most valuable commodity he had, and the real value of having a team of experts was that he could spend his time with the people he loved, doing the things he cared about.

And just look at Jesse and Cheryl. They just didn't know they could dream a bigger dream. They had no idea that what they had saved separately was enough for them to live a little more easily and even dream a little bigger! After purchasing their small RV, which they named "Rover," they still, to this day, travel as often as possible to all the beautiful parks in our beloved United States. "Now," I kiddingly say, "I have to chase them down to get them to review their financial plan each year." Their response is always, "We are just having too much fun, and we are confident you are taking care of us."

Fact #2 I've Shown You the BFS Way.

It is an easy three-step process that gets you thinking about your ideal life while providing us with your current financial picture. The fact is it takes extraordinarily little time for you to gather the information that we need to help you find solutions. You then sit back while we bring it all together in a plan that uncovers strategies for allowing your money to work for you, achieving your best life throughout your Go-Go, Slow-Go, and No-Go Years.

Fact #3 You Don't Need Permission; You Have Control.

Yes, you have the power to say, "No, I am not going to try and do this all myself." And "Yes, my time is more valuable than using it to sit in front of my computer trying to figure out what I have missed with regards to my money." "No, I don't have to work in a job that I no longer enjoy," and as the colonel would say, "Yes, I will let *you* do all of

the work. I can delegate what I am not an expert at." And so, you can.

Fact #4 The Time Is Now.

You won't get any closer to realizing your ideal life without starting to plan for it. It's just that simple. If you are not on track to achieving your goals, then the sooner you know that the sooner you can make the changes necessary to get you on track.

If you do have the assets required to provide financial independence, then it is time to confirm that they are invested in a fashion that will provide financial security for your lifetime, no matter what curveballs loom ahead.

If you own a business and don't have a succession plan in place, your entire legacy could be in trouble. So often, business owners have all their financial eggs in one basket and no real plan to unwind and get out when the time comes, either by choice or by no fault of their own. If you plan for it now, you can rest assured and be confident that you won't be forced to hang on too long. But if you don't have a plan, the stress could drive you to an early grave.

And you can be assured that your family will know that you loved them by leaving a well-thought-out estate plan that will provide for their financial, as well as emotional, wellbeing. We don't know when they will need this assistance, but the time is now for getting the planning done and the procedures in place.

Fact #5 It May Cost You More to Do Nothing.
As you saw in Janet and Kurt's case, it often pays to hire an expert. Having someone reviewing your total picture without emotion or preconceived notions is priceless when trying to get real answers. There are costs to hiring an advisor, but there could be greater costs by not hiring one.

An advisor who has your best interests at heart, as well as extensive knowledge of the current tax laws and market conditions, will cost much less than an uncoordinated "DIY" plan that has run off track and is destined to fail.

I would pose that the brilliance of this process is twofold. 1) It will allow you to pursue your emotional aspirations, giving you a real platform from which to achieve your dreams, and 2) It also provides the logic behind the emotion, the foundation of facts supporting the precise details required to afford the life you want to live. You don't have to be the expert. All you need to do is understand your "Why," and be able to relay it to your expert.

CHAPTER 10

*Delivering the painting is the most rewarding aspect of my entire process.
It often comes as a very emotional moment, one that brings me great anxiety.
What if something is just not right? What if I tried and missed? What if the loved
one expected more or something totally different?*

*But as the moment develops, I begin to see the tears, the signs of love, and the
look of awe in their expressions, and I know that I "found" the true person,
who is now looking back at us from the canvas.*

*I get to enjoy this same "moment of truth" experience when I am able to assure
my client that they can achieve financial security and live the life
they were meant to live.*

There is nothing more rewarding.

CHAPTER 10

So, What's in It for You?

You, Too, Can Live the Life You Envisioned!

FIVE YEARS AGO, Lynn would have never envisioned herself sitting at a dinner table on an island located on the southernmost point of the US. As she drank her coffee, she sat back in her chair, taking comfort in listening to the lighthearted chatter, and thought, *I can't believe I made it here. I feel like I am living in a dream that I never want to wake up from.*

As she looked around at the candlelit faces, she felt elated that *she* was included as one of the guests at the table. Each face was filled with beautiful expressions and character lines, derived from years of working through their previous lives. Many enjoyed their working years, but all felt they had earned a sort of "rite of passage" to try something new, focusing on more than just earning money. **Five years ago, she would not have been able to relate to these people. Today, she was one of them.**

Lynn had owned her own plumbing company, had fifty employees, and worked endless hours. She had married young but never found time for children or her husband, and after her divorce, she remained single for many years, focusing on the business, which became quite successful.

One day, Lynn woke up and decided she had had enough. She just didn't want one more employee issue, one more shipping mix-up, one more demanding customer. She didn't know what she wanted, but it wasn't this. Within two weeks, she put her business up for sale and called me.

Lynn had been a client for many years and thus had some idea that financially she could make this work. My job was to help her through the logistics while she decided what her next life would look like. Once she sold her business, she started realizing that she could be anyone, do anything, and live anywhere she wanted.

However, there was one challenge, and that was that her identity had changed. Even more, she wasn't sure she had one. She had always been the business owner, the boss, the one that made it all happen. Now, she needed to find a new identity.

This came over time, but since then, she has often said to me, **"I wish I had lived my working years differently, with some balance cultivating some other interests along the way. I wouldn't have been so lost at first, trying to find myself as a free person."**

Today, Lynn is a different woman. She smiles easily and dresses in brightly colored clothing that fits her newfound shape, which is fifty pounds lighter than before. She met Jim, a boat captain, on a trip to the Keys, and they have been inseparable ever since. She is part of a family and has meaningful, fulfilling relationships with people. **Now her money is working for her, while she is focusing on living.**

Accept the Gift of Guidance.
Don't wish you had done it sooner.

How to Get Started with Your Plan

If you feel it is finally time to *invest in yourself* and start planning for your ideal life, all you have to do is take the following steps:

The first thing you will want to do is to go to the Bonus page located at BeckFS.com/Bonus.8.htm.

Step 1: Schedule Your Discovery Meeting
First, you'll want to schedule your Free Personal Discovery meeting, where you can interview us, and we can get to know you to see if the BFS Way is in line with what you have been looking for. You can schedule your meeting by going to **BeckFS.com/Bonus.8.htm** or by calling our office at 317-547-1200.

Step 2: Complete Your BFS Way Discovery Questionnaire
This is the first step in helping us (and you) discover your life wishes, concerns, regrets, and achievements. We will go over this questionnaire together during our Discovery meeting. (See chapter 7 for a list of good questions to ask when interviewing an advisor candidate.)

Step 3: Complete the BFS Financial Factfinder
After we have discussed your current picture and future priorities, you will be provided with all of the pertinent disclosure documents. If you have decided to move forward with a plan, you will be furnished with the Financial Planning Agreement and quoted a fee for service. You will also be invited to complete the BFS Financial Factfinder.

Step 4: Get Enrolled in Your Personal BFS Money Site
You will receive an invitation to begin setting up your BFS Money Site and will be asked to schedule a follow-up data meeting to ensure your information is accurate and complete. We also can begin linking your accounts to your private BFS Money Site, enabling you to view all your accounts in real-time and in one place.

Step 5: Meet with Nancy and Learn about Your Solutions
You will meet with me either in person or through Zoom to review your complete financial plan. The plan will provide guidance in the areas of cash management, insurance, and risk, tax, and retirement planning, as well as estate and investment allocation reports.

If required, we may review various "what-if" scenarios that will help you better envision all your financial opportunities. At the end of the meeting, you will find a full PDF copy of your financial plan report in your Secure Vault/ Reports File located on your BFS Money Site.

If any implementation or additional planning is required, additional meetings may be scheduled at no additional cost for up to one year from the date of the initial planning agreement.

Plan More. Play More. Be More.

My hope is that this book has enlightened you to an easy way forward in addressing all your fears, desires, and apprehensions about financial planning and has instilled the realization that you deserve to have a team of trusted advisors to take away the day-to-day burden of financial planning so that you can focus on the life you want to live.

I believe that if you *Plan More*, you will have the time to *Play More*, which allows you to *Be More*.

Now, let's get started on your masterpiece.

"You can't go back and change the beginning,
but you can start where you are and change the ending."
—Unknown

EPILOGUE

SOME TIME AGO, I surveyed my clients, asking them to describe what new elements they found in their lives now that they had delegated the burden of financial planning to us. The list was longer than I had ever imagined! I received more than just yes and no answers, more than just one-sentence replies. I was astonished by the replies and the passion in their detailed written answers. I was on to something, and I wanted to share it.

Normally the topic of financial planning is perceived as uninspiring, burdensome, and intimidating. I know now, through the words of my clients, that the outcome can bring discovery, permission, enlightenment, joy, freedom, confidence, fulfillment, interrelationships, wisdom, gratitude, and yes, even grace. Now that is inspiring and worth sharing!

These were the very words my clients used to describe their transition from worrying about money to uncovering their "Why." I encourage you to consider their list of lasting effects that **Planning to Play the BFS Way** provided them and could instill in your own life.

Discovery. You'll find wonderful new discoveries about yourself and your new life that will bring you growth and more happiness. If you're like many, it will be the first time you've gone "excavating," and who knows what treasures you might find.

Permission. You will begin to allow yourself to consider new possibilities and to realize that you can, and do, deserve to start living the life you have worked so hard to save for. Giving yourself permission to enjoy your money is one of the hardest realizations most of us struggle with. When we finally can say, "It's time," it's forever life changing.

Enlightenment. You will begin to find out new things about yourself, new abilities, and even new Play List items that you never thought you'd consider before. These can seem like little light bulbs going off in your head, often at the most unexpected moments. The key is to be open to the "light" in your en*light*enments when they come.

Joy. With each new epiphany, you will be filled with delight and gratification that only comes when you listen and act on your own personal passions. Joy starts within you but then weaves its way into the world like a vine, starting out slowly and muted, and turning into something jubilant.

Freedom. Having flexibility and full control of your time is a privilege many never take. It doesn't really matter if they are quiet moments, last-minute moments, or well-thought-out moments, as long as they are *your* moments. Having the freedom to choose what you do with your moments is, for many, *everything*.

Confidence. Having a plan brings you the confidence required to let go and start enjoying the fruits of your labors. Knowing that your plan is secure will give you the courage to move on with the important things, leaving the everyday management to the experts.

Fulfillment. That sense of fulfillment that you have achieved something worthwhile during all those years you worked hard to save is a stunning realization. It is a very new emotion for many who have lived years either totally unfulfilled or with a muted sense of fulfillment.

Interrelationships. I have been amazed at the stories I hear from clients once they learn to let go and really start enjoying their family and friends. Spousal relationships, previously in trouble, are renewed. Friends begin to see you as someone they want to gravitate to, now that there is "*just something different about you.*" They want what you have.

Wisdom. Wisdom comes in many forms, and the meaning can include intelligence, foresight, and experience. But consider this: Those who are most wise have a voracious appetite for learning new things and are willing to place themselves in situations just a bit out of their comfort zone. They have learned the art of being comfortable with the uncomfortable. I, for one, have never met a "wise" person who would say, "I'm done now; I've learned it all."

Gratitude. We know we should be grateful for all that we have, but sometimes that emotion doesn't come easily. For many, it takes time and lots of self-realization that happiness comes from within. When we are able to live our life on our own terms, this emotion bubbles up to the surface with ease and begins to show up in ways that are admirable and contagious when interacting with others.

Grace. Grace is when it all comes together in one doubtless, refined package, filled with beauty, elegance, and even spiritual enlightenment. It happens when all is right with your world. Life is ever-changing, and both good and bad events will happen. But grace can be ever-present in your journey if you let it.

******

Thank you for reading. Please share this book with anyone you feel needs some encouragement in finding their own ideal life. I will admit, it was hard to stop writing as this truly is my one great passion.

–Nancy L. Beck

Plan More * Play More * Be More

ENDNOTES

1 CNBC, Acorns, and SurveyMonkey, "Americans Are More Confident About Their Retirement Savings Now Versus Three Years Ago Pre-Trump, According to Invest in You Savings Survey." CNBC news release, April 1, 2019, https://www.cnbc.com/2019/04/01/americans-are-more-confident-about-their-retirement-savings-now-versus-three-years-ago-pre-trump-according-to-the-invest-in-you-savings-survey.html.

2 "Taking the DIY Route to Money Management Could Ruin You." Business Insider, October 5, 2012, https://www.businessinsider.com/personal-finance/when-to-be-your-own-money-manager-2012-10.

3 Based on MSCI All Country World Equity Index, Bloomberg Barclays Global Aggregate Bond Index YTD, as of 12/26/2020, per AssetMark PortfolioEngine report.

4 "Planning for Your Long-Term Care Needs," Indiana Long Term Care Insurance Program, State of Indiana, accessed April 24, 2021, https://www.in.gov/iltcp/.

5 Scott Witt et al., "Nursing Home Costs," SeniorLiving.org, updated March 4, 2021, https://www.seniorliving.org/nursing-homes/costs/.

6 Brad Breeding, "What Will Long Term Care Cost and How Long Will I Need It?" MyLifeSite, December 14, 2020, https://mylifesite.net/blog/post/what-will-long-term-care-cost-and-how-long-will-i-need-it/.

I am definitely—"Not Finished."

ABOUT THE AUTHOR

Nancy Beck is a CERTIFIED FINANCIAL PLANNER™ professional and began her career in the financial services industry in 1984. She is the founder of Beck Financial Strategies, an independent, fee-based financial planning firm located on the historic Ft. Benjamin Harrison Campus in Indianapolis, Indiana. Beck holds FINRA Series 6, 7, 63 & SIE securities licenses and Life & Health insurance licenses in various states. She is also registered as an Investment Advisor Representative.

Beck is a dynamic speaker and has been dedicated to enhancing financial education by providing a series of financial planning workshops for corporations, associations, and various 501(c)(3) organizations. She is also a federal retirement planning professional and provides benefits education and training for federal and civil service employees.

The organizations that sponsor these workshops find the programs to be some of the most popular in their employee and membership benefits packages. Nancy inspires and educates people on the benefits of financial planning and provides customized, full-service financial planning assistance to help people achieve their financial freedom.

Beck is a member of the FPA (Financial Planning Association), NAWBO (National Association of Women Business Owners), SHRM (Society of Human Resource Management), as well as the Lawrence Chamber of Commerce. She has served as an adjunct faculty member for the College for Financial Planning, Colorado. She has been quoted in the *Indianapolis Business Journal* and *The Indianapolis Star* and periodically writes articles for various local newspapers.

Beck is also an award-winning portrait and plein air (in which works of outdoor scenes are created live onsite) artist. Her work has been accepted in the prestigious Indianapolis Hoosier Salon, from which she received a purchase award for one of her portraits. You will find her art exhibited in various galleries in the Florida Keys, in Indianapolis, and on her website, **www.NancyBeckFineArt.com**. Additionally, one of her paintings is exhibited in the permanent collection of The Truman Little White House Museum (in Key West, Florida) after winning the 2016 Plein Air Competition.

She and her husband, John, have been avid world travelers, seeking locations where they can ride bikes and where she can paint *en plein air*. Since the pandemic, however, they have focused their touring within the United States in their RV, which they endearingly refer to as "ET"

(for "Expensive Toilet"). The name was inspired by one of her clients.

Nancy is also an amateur musician and always has one of her much-loved ukuleles or guitars ready to play with friends and colleagues she meets while biking and traveling. Playing music reminds her to "Play More" in general, a motto she tries to instill in the minds of her clients as well.

"Life is short and sometimes taken a bit too seriously," she often says. *"We work to develop financial solutions for our clients that will enable them to use their money for the things that are important to them. 'Play More' might sound a little trite, but if we don't remind ourselves to enjoy life while we can, we often never will."*

Nancy provides financial services for clients throughout the country. She and her husband reside in Indianapolis, Indiana, and also on the quintessential *Love Lane* in Key West, Florida.

Invite Nancy to speak at your organization's upcoming meeting.

Visit the Beck Financial Strategies website at **www.BeckFS.com**

Contact her at **https://www.beckfs.com/contact_us/**

Visit her on Facebook at: **https://www.facebook.com/BeckFS**

Visit her on LinkedIn at: **https://www.linkedin.com/company/beck-financial-strategies/**

Visit her art website at **www.NancyBeckFineArt.com**

ACKNOWLEDGMENTS

I WOULD LIKE to acknowledge and thank the following people for giving me the ultimate gifts of their time, love, and encouragement so that I could write this book and achieve one of my own Play List goals.

I want to thank Elizabeth (Beth) Drury for her support and encouragement in writing this book and her steadfast commitment to the wellbeing of all of our Beck Financial Strategies clients. I hope that I can repay this encouragement as she writes her own book, which is currently in progress. I can't wait to see what she will do next, and I have no doubt it will be outstanding!

I want to thank my friends and clients who entrusted me with their life experiences, which helped me develop the real-life, but somewhat altered characters in this book. For obvious reasons, identities had to be changed, and facts needed to be altered just enough to be unrecognizable. But your inspirations and truths were behind every story I shared.

I would also like to thank my friends and family for putting up with me during this unrelenting process. Thank you for the hours of proofreading, brainstorming, and even traipsing through the snow to get into our house to photograph some of my artwork for this book. That goes way beyond the call of duty, and I am incredibly grateful!

I also want to mention the supportive and responsive team at J.W. Cole Financial. They have been an extraordinary business partner, always putting the needs of my clients and business first. I want to call out a *thank you* to all who have inspired me as a business owner with your conscientious and ethical culture of putting us first. This company knows its "Why" and does, in fact, help us build better businesses.

I would also like to thank the founder of Niche Pressworks, Nicole Gebhardt, for her unrelenting guidance in helping me draft the message I wanted to instill and for giving me the confidence that my voice was one that others would want to listen to, learn from, and be inspired by.

And last, I want to thank my aunt, Rosemary Browne Beck (otherwise fondly known as "FA," for "Favorite Aunt"). She has inspired me in both art and in writing by sharing her incredible artistic wisdom with me for many years and by sending handwritten letters complete with word games, rhymes, and wonderful short stories every month, always finding us wherever we are. My image of her sharing precious moments with her great-grandson is portrayed on the cover and in Chapter 2.

FINAL NOTE
THE POWER OF A PORTRAIT

I WAS VERY FORTUNATE to grow up around accomplished professional artists: my mother, Barbara Beck, who only started painting later in life; my aunt Rosemary Browne Beck; and my uncle Richard E. Beck, fondly known as Dick to many and "F.U." to me for "Favorite Uncle." All were the real thing, who earned numerous awards and recognition throughout their art careers.

My Uncle Dick, or "F.U.", encouraged me to paint portraits and would sit with me in my studio while I worked to give me pointers on my composition, color, shapes and most importantly—the light. Dick had been the art director for Eli Lilly and Company in Indianapolis for many years and he knew about art.

This book was finished and in the final stage when I came upon a letter that my aunt Rosemary wrote just after my uncle passed away. I felt compelled to share it along with a portrait that she painted of him many years ago. "F.U." would have loved that I wrote this book, and from wherever he is, I hope that his ingenious eye for design would be pleased with the result.

THE PORTRAIT - *written by Rosemary Browne Beck*

I painted a portrait of Dick in 1999. For some reason, I didn't like it and gave it a poorly-lit wall in the basement studio.

For Dick's funeral, someone put it on an easel close to the entrance of the chapel. When alone afterwards and putting things in order, I placed it on a chair in the bedroom to look at closely. The portrait had become alive for me. How could brushstrokes have this power? Without words, he was telling me about beauty. No words could have told it the way his near flexible lips and flesh projected it. (Maybe I was tired and susceptible.) It was so opposite to the helplessness in which he left us. It's as if he'd converted that hopeless fluidity into a gel of vigor and transferred it to me.

I sat and listened for what seemed about half an hour. I wish I could put it into our fragile language, the strength and optimism which has faded a little bit—but still remains in my spirits like a beacon close by.

Love, from Rosemary

FIND YOUR **LIFE** WORTH LIVING

SIGN UP NOW FOR YOUR 1-HOUR PERSONAL DISCOVERY SESSION

During Our Time We Will:

Review Your BFS Personal Discovery Questionnaire

Explore Your "Play More" Goals and Opportunities

Analyze Your Current Portfolio Strengths/Weaknesses

Discuss Our BFS "Under-One-Roof" Advisor Model

Create a Gap Analysis of Your Existing Plan

SCHEDULE YOUR DISCOVERY MEETING TODAY

With the Founder of Beck Financial Strategies and
Author of *The Art of the Plan*, Nancy Beck, CFP®

Call (317) 547-1200 or Visit BeckFS.com/Bonus.8.htm

WORRY LESS & PLAY MORE

THE EASY BFS WAY

KNOW YOU'RE STAYING ON TRACK WITH YOUR OWN PERSONAL BFS MONEY SITE

Monitor Your Net Worth

Track Your Investments

Securely Store Important Documents

Provide Easy Access to Loved Ones

Ensure Your Plan Remains on Track

Enhance Time Freedom to "Play More"

GET ACCESS to the TOOLS you need to transition into THE LIFE YOU WANT TO LIVE

Learn more about the BFS Money Site at
BeckFS.com/Bonus.8.htm

CPSIA information can be obtained
at www.ICGtesting.com
Printed in the USA
BVHW010346081121
621056BV00003B/187